YOU COULDN'T MAKE IT UP

Richard Littlejohn was born in 1954, white,
male and in Essex. (In twenty years' time
any baby answering to that description will
be found hidden in the bulrushes.) He has
been in journalism all his working life,
recently writing controversial columns for
the *Evening Standard*, the *Sun* and the *Daily
Mail*. In 1993 he won the *What The Papers
Say* 'Irritant of the Year' award. He has also
presented his own shows on LBC Radio,
Sky TV and LWT.

Richard Littlejohn

YOU COULDN'T MAKE IT UP

Mandarin

A Mandarin Paperback
YOU COULDN'T MAKE IT UP

First published in Great Britain 1995
by William Heinemann Ltd
This edition published 1996
by Mandarin Paperbacks
an imprint of Reed International Books Ltd
Michelin House, 81 Fulham Road, London SW3 6RB
and Auckland, Melbourne, Singapore and Toronto

Copyright © Richard Littlejohn 1995
The author has asserted his moral rights

A CIP catalogue record for this title
is available from the British Library
ISBN 0 7493 1978 X

Typeset by Deltatype Ltd, Ellesmere Port, Cheshire
Printed and bound in Great Britain by BPC Paperbacks Ltd
A member of the British Printing Company Ltd

To My Mum and Dad

CONTENTS

Acknowledgements

I would like to thank those editors who have had faith in me, and provided support and inspiration, primarily the late John Leese, at the *Evening Standard*, Kelvin McKenzie and Stuart Higgins at the *Sun*, and Paul Dacre at the *Daily Mail*. The themes in this book have been explored in those newspapers over the years, with a cavalier disregard for taste, decency, and the feelings of the great and the good. I would also like to thank all those without whom this book would not have been possible – especially David Mellor, Lady Di, Prince Charles, John Major, Haringey Council, the Commission for Racial Equality, and the *Guardian*. They have contributed enormously to the gaiety of the nation.

INTRODUCTION

I was born in 1954, white, male and in Essex. In twenty years' time any baby answering that description will be found hidden in the bullrushes. I'm assumed to be racist, sexist and philistine, someone to be shunned at all times by politically-correct company. In the London Borough of Haringey, where I have lived for the past ten years, white men from Essex are about the only minority without their own council support unit, community centre and army of dedicated social workers. We don't count. Multi-culturalism doesn't embrace the cultural pursuits of white men from Essex. I can remember telling a Guyanese friend last summer that I was planning to spend an idyllic day watching cricket at Southend, sipping Ridley's ales and feasting on Rossi's ice cream and fish and chips wrapped in the *Essex Chronicle*. I used to spend many happy days at Southend cricket ground as a child. My grandad was a member and my dad ran the car park on his days off from the railway. My friend started playing air violin and making the sound of a cat being castrated with a rusty Stanley knife, laughing at my sentimentality. 'Hang on a minute,' I said. 'I've been in your office and seen the rows of Back to Africa books. You're not the only one with roots. You might have Kunte Kinte, but we've got Trevor Bailey.'

Multi-culturalism means never having to say you're

sorry – unless, of course, you happen to be a white man from Essex. Then you're expected to spend your life apologising simply for being born. The fact that you have no choice in the matter is irrelevant. Yet 'culture' is used to excuse all kinds of anti-social and intolerable behaviour, from burning books and issuing death threats against authors to mutilating children and slaughtering goats in the street. That's all perfectly permissible. But try selling a jar of home-made jam at a jumble sale and the full weight of the law will descend upon you. It is now a criminal offence for a publican to sell a customer a pint of shandy. By the time this book is published it will be a criminal offence for one Englishman to sell another Englishman a pound of apples. We are all criminals now.

Schools which have given up teaching children how to read and write bar Christmas on the grounds that it is racist. British fishermen are forced by law to sit in port while foreign vessels plunder our traditional fishing grounds. Rapacious executives turn themselves into overnight millionaires, pillaging monopoly utilities which used to belong to us all. And the majority of people in this country are left fuming impotently on the sidelines.

I've been a journalist since 1971 and a columnist since 1988. I've spent much of that time railing against the insanities imposed upon us by those whom we elect and pay to protect our interests. I am not a politician. To borrow a phrase from Billy Bragg, I don't want to change the world, I'm not looking for a new England. I was quite happy with the one we had. It is the job of a columnist to sit at the back and throw bottles, to ridicule, to draw attention to the lunacy being enacted in our name.

This book contains example after example of the madness of the system. If I had sat down twenty years ago – even ten years ago – and written it as a work of fiction I would have been laughed out of court. Sometimes it is simply impossible to stay ahead of the game. Time and again I have let my imagination run wild, trying to predict the next absurd development – to poke fun – only to find that reality has beaten me to it. The evidence is contained in this book.

You couldn't make it up.

London
Spring 1995

SNOUTS IN THE TROUGH

Only in Britain could the part–time chairman of a monopoly company announce profits of £1.25 billion and then complain about the weather. If it hadn't been for the warm winter British Gas would have made another £135 million, in 1994, directors grumbled when they presented their annual report. If only it had snowed, then we'd have had to turn up the thermostat and chief executive Cedric Brown wouldn't be struggling to get by on a derisory £435,000 a year. Still, when you're raking in profits of £40–a–second it helps explain why Cedric couldn't understand why we were all getting so worked up about his fat salary and treble share options all round. In the context of £1.25 billion, his remuneration package doesn't amount to a round of drinks. I don't know how these people manage to keep a straight face. Especially as British Gas is shedding 25,000 staff, has reduced spending on safety checks, closed showrooms and announced that customers who insist on only paying for gas they've actually used when the bill arrives will be charged more than those who sign a direct debit mandate allowing the company to dip into their bank account at will.

The news of the British Gas bonanza came the day after it was revealed that Northern Electricity consumers have been over–charged to the tune of £380 each because of the failure of the industry's price regulation system. And if Northern Electricity has been getting away with it, you can bet your next bill that the other electricity companies have too. Privatisation was meant to free the state monoliths from bureaucratic control for the benefit of all. And there's no denying that many of the companies have become more efficient and more customer-responsive. But the sub-plot has been the venal way in which those who run the companies have been lining their own pockets. It was revealed in February that the chairman of the National Grid stands to make £2 million from share options when the sale of the electricity generating industry is complete.

The kind of pay rises and share options the other heads of former nationalised industries have awarded themselves are well documented – anything up to 300 per cent salary increases and options worth millions of pounds. All for doing the same job they were doing when the companies were in the public sector. Still, we shouldn't have expected anything else once the nationalised industries joined the market economy. None have done more to bring capitalism into disrepute than the leading capitalists themselves. We shouldn't begrudge risk-takers and those who shoulder the burden of responsibility for organisations with thousands of employees and multi-million-pound turnovers fair reward. But all the evidence of the past few years has been that the rewards have been out of all proportion to achievement. Executives have written themselves 'Heads we win, tails we win' contracts. Even if the companies they are responsible for go down the gurgler, the man at the top normally jumps out with a golden parachute bag full of used notes to cushion his landing. The instances of this kind of abuse are widespread enough to warrant a book of their own. There is no more glaring example of the way in which privatisations which were supposed to benefit us all have enriched the men in the boardroom, than the report from the National Consumer Council, which concludes that consumers have been ripped off to the tune of £1 billion since the water companies were removed from public ownership. The sort of man who was happy to accept annual remuneration in the region of £50,000 when he was working in the public sector has now made himself wealthy beyond his wildest dreams. The salary of the chairman of Severn Trent, for instance, has increased from £51,000 pre-privatisation to £302,000. That does not include £200,000 worth of share options. The chairmanship of the Thames Water Company, which was valued at £41,000 per annum in 1989, had ballooned to £317,000 by the middle of 1994. Meanwhile, water bills, which used to constitute a minuscule item of household expenditure, have increased in some parts of the country by up to 150 per cent. It is a national disgrace.

Executive pay leapt to the top of the political agenda in 1994 and 1995. But I have been drawing attention to this ticking timebomb for years. Indeed a few years ago, I dreamed up a spoof game show which I called 'Snouts In The Trough'.

'Now we go over live to the CBI ballroom in London for tonight's edition of "Snouts In The Trough". Here is your host, Mr Greedy himself, Lee-ee Pemberton.'

PEMBERTON: Welcome to 'Snouts In The Trough', the game show which does for company chairmen what Littlewoods does for pools winners. Please say hello to my lovely personal assistant, everyone's executive toy, Miss Five Times A Night, the lovely Fiona!

AUDIENCE: OINK, OINK, OINK, OINK.

PEMBERTON: Settle down, settle down. Where do you think you are: The Institute of Directors? Fiona, my love, who is tonight's lucky contestant on 'Snouts In The Trough'?

FIONA: Hoping to get his snout in the trough tonight is Mr George Grasping, from Milton Friedman, in Hampshire.

PEMBERTON: George Grasping, COME ON DOWN!

AUDIENCE: OINK, OINK, OINK, OINK!

PEMBERTON: Now then George, tell us a little about yourself.

GRASPING: I am forty-seven years old, chairman of United Urinals Plc and my ambition is to quadruple my salary.

PEMBERTON: You've come to the right place, George. Last week, the chairman of North West Water took home £144,000 and the week before that the chairman of British Gas helped himself to £370,000, two houses and over £200,000 worth of electrical appliances.

AUDIENCE: OINK, OINK, OINK, OINK!

PEMBERTON: The rules are very simple. Every time you answer a question correctly you get a massive pay rise. So get ready to play 'Snouts In The Trough'!

AUDIENCE: OINK, OINK, OINK, OINK!

PEMBERTON: Right, George. An easy question to start with, just to relax you. How is a typical chairman's pay determined?

GRASPING: By an independent panel of non-executive directors, Lee.

PEMBERTON: Correct, you have got £20,000.

AUDIENCE: OINK, OINK, OINK, OINK!

PEMBERTON: And for £40,000, who appoints the non-executive directors?

GRASPING: The chairman, Lee.

PEMBERTON: You are absolutely right.

AUDIENCE: OINK, OINK, OINK, OINK!

PEMBERTON: For £80,000, what do those independent directors have to pay the chairman?

GRASPING: The market rate.

PEMBERTON: Correct!

AUDIENCE: OINK, OINK, OINK, OINK!

PEMBERTON: Now, George, take your time. Imagine you are negotiating with the trades unions. Your employees want a pay rise in line with inflation. How do you react?

GRASPING: I tell them we are in a recession and we cannot pay ourselves more than we earn.

PEMBERTON: You have just won £160,000 a year.

AUDIENCE: OINK, OINK, OINK, OINK!

PEMBERTON: Suppose profits and sales are down, what do you do?

GRASPING: Sack half the workforce, Lee?

PEMBERTON: I'm afraid I'm going to need a little more than that, George.

GRASPING: Er, sack half the workforce, cut wages on the shopfloor, give myself a £50,000 pay rise and buy new Jags for all the directors.

PEMBERTON: Spot on, George. You now have £320,000 a year.

AUDIENCE: OINK, OINK, OINK, OINK!

PEMBERTON: Next question. Your sales director is a hopeless old drunk and fiddling his expenses. But he is a freemason and a member of your golf club. What do you do?

GRASPING: I give him a £500,000 golden handshake, £2000-a-week pension and fix him up with a new job as a director of a company run by another member of my lodge.

PEMBERTON: George, you have just won yourself a new record salary of £640,000!

AUDIENCE: OINK, OINK, OINK, OINK!

PEMBERTON: Super, super! The £640,000 is safe. Do you want to go on for tonight's star prize of a LIFE PEERAGE?

AUDIENCE: OINK, OINK, OINK, OINK!

GRASPING: I'm going for the big one, Lee.

PEMBERTON: Good choice, George. Fiona, if you'd like to take George into the soundproof sauna cabin. Now, I can't give you any assistance on this, George, so take your time. Fiona will help you relax. I must take your first answer, so listen carefully.

Your salary has been widely criticised in the Press and on television. Questions have been asked in the Commons. What would you do?

GRASPING: I'd appoint a member of the Cabinet as a non-executive director and make a donation of £1 million to the Conservative Party.

PEMBERTON: Arise LORD GRASPING!

AUDIENCE: OINK, OINK, OINK, OINK!

PEMBERTON: Didn't he do well? Don't forget to tune in at the same time next week when we'll be joined by another group of company chairmen hoping to get their SNOUTS IN THE TROUGH!

It's interesting looking back four years later how the ending anticipated yet another scandal. The inclination of most Conservative MPs has not been to try to derail this runaway Orient Express of a gravy train but to clamber on board. If there was one single issue, apart from Europe, which dominated the political agenda in 1994, it was the way in which Tory MPs were sticking their snouts in the trough. Leaving aside the arrogance and incompetence, what will finally destroy this Conservative Government is the un-ashamed spivvery. The MPs For Hire scandal, which erupted following the revelation that two Tory members were apparently willing to ask questions in the House, and were offered £1000 from a fictitious company invented by the *Sunday Times* as encouragement, is merely the scab on the boil. The abiding image of the Major administration is that of a bunch of Brylcreemed gangsters sticking their elephantine trunks in a trough of their own creation. We are dealing with a collection of people who – in the memorable expression of my former editor, Kelvin Mackenzie – would sell their arses in Simpson's window. The Register of Members' Interests reads like the menu of an upmarket massage parlour: 'I'm an MP, Buy Me'. The only difference between the Tory MPs David Tredinnick and Graham Riddick and the rest of their colleagues is that the company from which they took their bung was fictitious, dreamt up by the *Sunday Times*.

Take, at complete random, Sir Michael Grylls, the Conservative member for North West Surrey. He has the following list of directorships and consultancies in the Register of Members' Interests:

> Le Carbon Lorraine (GB) Ltd
> Cape PLC
> Columbus Holdings Ltd
> Electrophoretics PLC
> Charter PLC
> The Association of Authorised Public Accountants
> The Unitary Tax Campaign
> Digital Equipment Co Ltd
> National Federation of Post Office and BT Pensioners
> Ian Greer Associates

Were I resident in North West Surrey, I would like to know where he finds the time for all these extracurricular responsibilities. He was returned to parliament to represent all of his constituents, even those who did not vote for him. It should be a full-time job. He was elected as the member of North West Surrey. He was not elected as the member for Le Carbon Lorraine (GB). Grylls is a glaring example, there are plenty more. The worst of the lot are the former ministers now sitting on the boards of former nationalised industries which they themselves helped return to the private sector. That's quite apart from all their other directorships and consultancies.

It all came to a head around the time of the launch of the National Lottery. Now you can rant and rave all you like, write tendentious editorials, or you can ridicule. I've always found ridicule the most effective weapon. When the MPs

For Hire scandal reached its peak, I decided to tie it all in with the National Lottery.

'Welcome to the first ever draw in the new National Lootery. We're crossing live now to the Palace of Westminster to join our hosts, Ronny Greed and Billy Bung.'

GREED: Hello, good evening and what's your Swiss bank account number?

BUNG: Welcome to the ultimate supermarket sweep.

GREED: Yes indeed. All you have to do to enter is get yourself elected as a Member of Parliament.

BUNG: We've a whole host of star prizes to give away tonight. Plenty of lucrative directorships and consultancies with some lucky MPs' names on. So let's make that draw.

GREED: The first name out of the barrel tonight is Neville Trotter, from Tynemouth.

BUNG: I wonder if he's any relation of Derek Trotter, from New York, Paris and Peckham?

GREED: Could be. He's certainly got a lot in common with Del Boy.

BUNG: Well, Mr Trotter, your reward for becoming an MP is a grand total of six consultancies.

GREED: Yes, indeed, Neville, your membership of the House of Commons has won you nice little earners from the following companies:

AMEC Offshore Ltd
Bowring Group
British Marine Equipment
British Transport Police
Go Ahead Northern
Grant Thornton
Total value . . . SIXTY THOUSAND POUNDS!

BUNG: Pigs win prizes, that's our motto. Trotter, pigs, geddit?

GREED: So get those snouts in the trough.

BUNG: Our next winner tonight is Tim Yeo, from Suffolk.

GREED: Mr Yeo wins dinner for two in London's trendy Langan's Brasserie with a tasty Tory councillor from Hackney.

BUNG: Give her one for me, my son. Well done.

GREED: More consultancies to give away, Billy. The next lucky boy is Patrick Nicholls, from Teignbridge.

BUNG: Paddy baby, you've won big bunce from the following firms:

> British Shops Stores Association
> Channel Express Ltd
> Federation of Associations of Specialist and
>   Sub-Contractors
> Hill & Smith Holdings
> Howard de Walden Estates
> Port Enterprises Ltd
> Waterfront Partnerships
> National Sub-Contractors Council
> Wells Tailors

Never mind the quality, feel the width. What's that little lot worth, Ronny?

GREED: A staggering NINETY THOUSAND POUNDS!

BUNG: Didn't he do well?

GREED: He did, Billy, he did. But not as well as our star prizewinner tonight.

BUNG: You don't mean?

GREED: Yes I do. He's done it again. I'm talking about the luckiest man in Britain.

BUNG: Yes, he's made more money out of the Commons than any other MP currently sitting in the House.

GREED: He's an example to all aspiring Tory backbenchers on how to milk the system and turn disgrace into hard cash.

BUNG: Yes, indeed, ladies and gentlemen. We're talking about Mr Sleaze himself.

GREED: And we're delighted to say he's here with us tonight. Yes, he's agreed to take his snout out of the trough for five minutes to be our very special guest.

BUNG: In exchange for only £10,000.

GREED: That's our boy.

BUNG: He's worked hard to get where he is today. We are talking sleaze beyond the call of duty.

GREED: Indeed we are. No simple questions here. Our special guest tonight had to sleep with a gruesome old slapper and humiliate his wife and family in public.

BUNG: That's what I call dedication. But it was worth it, wasn't it?

GREED: It certainly was, Billy. Let's look at some of his consultancies:

> Abela Holdings
> Chesfield PLC
> Ernst & Young
> Investcorp Bank AC
> Middle East Economic Digest
> Middle Eastern Broadcasting Centre

BUNG: Not forgetting:

> Racal Tacticom Ltd
> Shandwick Consultants
> Short Brothers PLC
> AND
> Vosper Thorneycroft!

GREED: Or his own show on Radio 5, assorted television programmes and a column in the *Guardian*.

BUNG: Now we're talking really sleazy.

GREED: Our star prizewinner with total winnings of an astronomical THREE HUNDRED THOUSAND POUNDS!

BUNG: Will you welcome The Emperor, The Grand Master, The Almighty Ruler of Super Heavy Sleaze . . .

GREED: DAVID MELLOR, COME ON DOWN!

Sounds of police sirens. Presenters and contestants exit in direction of Venezuela.

I shall come on to Mellor later. He warrants an entire chapter all of his own. But there is an underlying theme here. What we are witnessing reminds me of the last months of the Second World War. Those who have profited most – and not always deservedly –from sixteen years of Conservative government are like the retreating Nazi generals. They have decided they are about to be overrun and are frantically stripping the loot, shipping it back to the bunker, blowing up the bridges and booking their tickets to Bolivia. They know once nice Mr Blair is installed in Downing Street the days of wine and share options will be over. This pillaging isn't only confined to the heads of the former nationalised industries. Elsewhere in the private sector, directors are embarking on slash-and-burn policies, sacking thousands of employees, closing factories and branch offices while the unions are still too weak to resist, jacking up prices and service charges before the regulators move in and giving themselves big pay increases before top tax rates rise to at least 50 per cent and the ceiling on National Insurance is lifted.

In the week in which we learned that the chairman of Nat West was to receive an extra £100,000, I discovered that my own branch manager had been told that he was now surplus to requirements after thirty-one years of loyal service – even though he is still in his forties. Services provided by the branch itself are being downgraded.

Tory MPs have looked at the opinion polls, looked at the Prime Minister, and looked around for other jobs. The reason so many of them are gathering directorships and consultancies like nuts in May is because very few of them expect to be in Parliament after the next election. I wonder if any of them lift their snouts long enough to reflect on the part they will have played in bringing about defeat?

INNAMEETIN

Much as the politicians must shoulder the lion's share of the blame for Britain's economic decline, a fair proportion of guilt must fall on the shoulders of so-called businessmen. I spent ten years of my life working as an industrial correspondent, coming into daily contact with many of the senior managers responsible for running our industries. And I was left with the impression that very few of them could run a bath, let alone a company with a multi-million-pound turnover. No one who has ever been to a Confederation of British Industry conference would invest a single penny piece in any of our leading companies. Although they pride themselves on being risk-takers, the greatest risk most of these senior managers have ever run is the risk of being caught shagging their secretaries in a seaside hotel where they are supposed to be attending a conference.

Let me give you an example. When I worked on the *Evening Standard* I went to cover a CBI conference in Bournemouth, which was being addressed by Labour's then industry spokesman – and subsequently leader – the late John Smith. Evening paper deadlines mean that reporters have to be up with the milk. In those days the latest copy for a first edition inside page – which was about all the CBI ever warranted – was around 8.30am. Lying in my hotel bedroom, with an advance of a speech due to be delivered by some CBI bigwig at 9.30am, warning of impending doom if ever there was to be another Labour government, I decided what was needed to spice up my story was a quote from John Smith. I'd seen him downstairs in the bar the previous evening and so reasoned that he must be staying in the same hotel. By then it was about 7.45am, not an unreasonable time to be calling a politician, I reckoned. With any luck, I might catch him before he headed downstairs for the full English breakfast. I called the switchboard and asked to be put through to Mr John Smith's room. The phone must have rung seven or eight times and I was just about to put it down when it was answered by a woman.

'Good morning. Could I speak to Mr Smith, please?'

'Er, who?'

'Mr Smith.'

'Mr Smith?'

'That's right, Mr John Smith. I have got the right room, haven't I?'

'Oh, Mr Smith. Mr John Smith. Er, yes, you have got the right room. I'll just wake him.'

'Hello,' said a bleary, unshaven male voice.

'Mr Smith?'

'Who?'

'Mr Smith.'

'Oh, er, yes, er, right, sorry.'

'Good morning, Mr Smith. This is Richard Littlejohn, from the *Standard*.'

'Standard?'

'Yes, the *Evening Standard* newspaper, in London.'

'What do you want?'

'Just a brief word, Mr Smith. A couple of quotes for the first edition.'

'How did you find me? How did you know I was here?'
'I saw you downstairs in the bar last night.'
Muffled silence.
'Mr Smith, are you still there?'
'Yes, er, how can I help you?'
'I just wanted reaction to this morning's speech.'
'I haven't heard it yet.'
'I've got an advance copy. In a nutshell, what it says is that a Labour government would be a disaster for British industry. I just wanted a couple of quotes from you.'
'Well, er, I would go along with that.'
'You would?'
'Yes, I think that Labour would introduce all kinds of regulations and we'd see a return to the days of trades union power which did so much damage during the 1970s.'

It was then that the penny dropped. The early-morning gruffness had cleared from the voice and what emerged was not the measured tones of an Edinburgh lawyer but the rounded vowels of the English Home Counties. I had not been connected to John Smith MP, but to a captain of industry batting for Britain with some doxy. He had obviously forgotten that he had booked into the hotel under the name of Mr and Mrs John Smith. I thanked him and terminated the conversation, collapsing convulsed with laughter on the bed. This poor sod obviously had visions of seeing himself plastered all over the newspapers. ACME WIDGETS BOSS SCREWS AND GETS HIS NUTS TIGHTENED or something. I tell you, you really couldn't make it up.

But back to my theme, although this wasn't as much a diversion as it might appear. Britain was once the world's greatest manufacturing and trading nation, founded on innovation, flair, risk, courage, skill and sweat. Men of vision built dynamic industries and assembled powerful engines of wealth-creation. There were always arguments about how that wealth was distributed. But even the hated mill owners and coal barons provided jobs, homes and food. Industrialists, engineers and scientists were national heroes, honoured for their towering contributions to the common good. Their invention and investment, their export achievements brought showers of knighthoods and peerages. They employed teams of 'boffins' in white coats to come up with new ideas, trained craftsmen to build what people wanted to buy at the right price. Salesmen scoured the globe for new markets. The world bought British. The British bought British. Businessmen were judged by what they made, what they sold, how many jobs they created, how many factories they opened. If they became rich, they earned it.

Today the heirs to the noble traditions of men like Morris, Cadbury, Lever and Austin are a bunch of two-bob spivs, interested only in lining their own pockets before they get found out. Their achievements are measured in terms of 'rationalisation', 'restructuring', 'asset maximisation' and 'strategic yield enhancement' – in other words, sacking people and closing things down. They sit in expensive restaurants congratulating each other on how many redundancies they have announced. Another bottle of Bollinger, old boy? Instead of hiring engineers and inventors and salesmen, they bring in teams of accountants and 'human resources' specialists. Instead of investing in ideas and people and products, they scour every nook and cranny for savings. The successful manager is the one who sacks the most people, sends out the most memos threatening disciplinary action against anyone who leaves his office light burning during lunchtime and makes staff sign forms in triplicate before they can get their hands on a Biro or a packet of paper clips. Directors appoint public relations managers on seventy grand a year to explain why craftsmen earning a quarter of that are being sacked and bring in teams of personnel experts on two grand a day to tell them why they should get rid of the tea lady. Rather than actually make anything, they concentrate on selling Australian coal to Newcastle, Belgian chocolates to Bournville, German steel to Sheffield and Japanese cars to Coventry. The marketing men are paid much more than the inventors and engineers. That's why the inventors and engineers go abroad.

Try calling a senior industrialist. You'll be told he's 'innameetin'. That's the trouble with British industry. They're always 'innameetin'. And if they're not 'innameetin', they're away at a conference, probably booked into a hotel under the name of John Smith.

WINNING THE LOTTERY WITHOUT BUYING A TICKET

I've never really understood the British attitude to money and success. The week the National Lottery started up, a satellite dish installer hit the jackpot to the tune of £839,000. Joy was unconfined. There was dancing in the street.

The brewery sent two kegs of beer to his local pub to help him celebrate. The Prime Minister sent his congratulations. Yet in the same week the head of one of the most profitable companies in the country got a £200,000 pay rise – taking him to £475,000 a year – and there was widespread outrage. MPs queued up to denounce his greed. Words like 'obscene' and 'grotesque' were sprayed about. Now Cedric Brown, the head of British Gas, isn't the best advert for capitalism. We resent his money because we don't think he has done anything to deserve it. And since the privatisation of the state utilities there has been an ugly rush by the men at the top to fill their boots. Three hundred per cent pay rises and treble share options all round.

There is a principle at stake here. Why is it that the salaries of leading businessmen come under critical scrutiny – indeed some are called before committees of the House of Commons to justify their earnings – yet no one gives a fig about a moronic, spotty youth with a back-to-front baseball cap earning millions from miming to a pop record? Or an emaciated bag of bones being paid twenty-five grand an hour for modelling a frock? Come to that, why is it they object to the chairman of British Gas being paid £475,000 a year but not to an actor being paid £100,000 for a couple of days' filming an advert for gas cookers?

Leave aside the former nationalised industries for a minute and consider the case of Peter Wood, founder of the Direct Line insurance company. Reaction to the news that he earned £18 million in a single year and had been bought out by the Royal Bank of Scotland to the tune of a further £24 million was a potent mixture of envy and spite. Labour politicians and left-wing commentators described his fortune as obscene – that word again – and demanded that people like him should have to pay more tax. That's a similar mentality to the plankton who can't pass an expensive car without running a key along the side of it. Even with a clever accountant, I would guess that Mr Wood will still have had to pay around £15 million in tax. That's not exactly small change. It should be more than enough to keep a fair few outreach co-ordinators, gollywog inspectors and grief counsellors in the manner to which they have become accustomed. Mr Wood has done a damned sight more for this country than any of those now slavering to get their hands on his money. Apart from cutting insurance bills, he has also created 9000 jobs in the teeth of a recession. That's 9000 people paying tax, National Insurance, VAT and a range of other duties. Of course, if you are struggling along on the average wage or even on the dole there may be a tendency to cast an envious eye at Mr Wood's millions and come to the conclusion that life's a bitch. But we shouldn't begrudge him a single penny. And if his fortune is 'obscene' I wonder what word those who call it that would use to describe a woman making love to a donkey? In the United States he would be a national hero – living proof that even if every little boy can't grow up to be president, he can become a millionaire. All it takes is one good idea and a bit of hard work. The Americans would say to themselves: 'If he can do it, so can I.' In Britain, plenty of folk think they could have achieved what Mr Wood has. But most of them couldn't because they are too stupid and lazy and think the world owes them a living. So the typical reaction was: to grudgingly concede that he had one good idea but then ask: 'What has he done to deserve all that money? Let's take it off him. Rich bastard.'

The politicians are always in the van of any moves to confiscate our money. They think they can spend it better than we can. It is worth remembering that it is our money. Governments don't have any money. All they do is think of different ways of wasting it. When you see politicians and lobbyists demanding more 'resources' for this and that, what they mean is they want to spend more of our money. You often see surveys indicating that people want to pay more tax. These are all rubbish. What people actually mean is that they want other people to pay more tax – successful people like Peter Wood, or anyone else who appears to have a few bob more than them. When higher taxes which affect everyone are levied –such as the poll tax or VAT on fuel – there are howls of protest.

Economic prosperity and full employment will not be achieved by putting up taxes. Politicians must kick the habit of spending our money like Imelda Marcos in a shoe shop. Real jobs are not created by hiring another few thousand NHS administrators. They are created by businessmen like Peter Wood. He has done far more for Britain than a satellite dish installer who got lucky or any of the politicians plotting to take his money away from him. We should be trying to emulate his success and wealth, not disparage them.

ORGASM AND GAITERS

Sporting the obligatory AIDS ribbon and looking like a cross between Charles Hawtrey and Wilfrid Brambell, the Rt Rev. Derek Rawcliffe, seventy-three-year-old Assistant Bishop of Ripon and former Bishop of Glasgow, came out of the closet and announced on national television that he is a homosexual.

Why?

If he had a predilection for wearing a nappy made out of BacoFoil or retiring for the evening with a satsuma in his mouth and a bin liner over his head, would he have felt obliged to share that with us, too? Frankly, I'm not in the slightest bit interested in what passions stir under his cassock. Or anyone else's, for that matter. What the clergy get up to in their own time is entirely a matter for them – unless of course they're taking more than a spiritual interest in the church cub pack or preaching the sins of adultery shortly before nipping round the back of the vestry for a spot of orgasm and gaiters with the wife of the local JP.

I have no objection to gay priests or to homosexuals in the armed forces, come to that. But then I'm not a practising member of the Church of England or responsible for maintaining discipline on board an aircraft carrier at sea for six months of the year. Instead of making such a song and dance about their sexuality, why don't priests such as

Bishop Rawcliffe simply join a church which is happy to accommodate them instead of trying to impose their morality on an unwilling majority of C of E worshippers who find homosexuality abhorrent? There must be a church in San Francisco which would welcome them with open arms. I'm sure God wouldn't mind. Whatever the Rev. Ian Paisley and the Pope might maintain, I shouldn't imagine God is a sectarian. I just don't want to read another word about them.

Similarly with gays in the military. I don't think homosexuality is incompatible with membership of the armed forces and, indeed, the rules making it an offence have now been changed, just as the rules governing pregnant servicewomen have also been changed. But when nurse Jeanette Smith joined the RAF she knew perfectly well that practising lesbianism was grounds for dismissal. That was the deal. She could simply have kept her sexuality to herself and provided she didn't spend her time chatting up the other nurses she would still be in her job. Women have for years lived with other women. Apart from the observation that one of them smoked a pipe and wore sensible shoes, no one pried into what they did behind the lace curtains.

These days, the Love That Dare Not Speak Its Name has become the Love That Can't Keep Its Mouth Shut. I am sick and tired of opening the newspapers every morning to be bombarded by proselytising homosexuals and lesbians. To be perfectly honest, I may be getting old, but I'm also sick and tired of reading about the heterosexual lives of MPs, pop stars and five-times-a-night stockbrokers. What is required is a moratorium on stories about sex, homo-, hetero-, extra-marital or otherwise. A period of silence. As they used to say in the music halls: 'I don't wish to know that. Kindly leave the stage.'

Meanwhile church leaders decided to drop the Cross

from their national advertising campaign for Easter after some clergy complained that such symbols are 'laden with too much cultural baggage'.

The Churches' Advertising Network said the Cross was inappropriate for a festival to celebrate Christ's Resurrection. Instead, posters for Holy Week at bus stops and on hoardings carried the following spiritual message: 'Surprise! said Jesus to his friends three days after they buried him.' Underneath, it read: 'To be continued at a Church near you.' I have never heard of the Churches' Advertising Network, but I have a vision of a group of men in designer dog collars, pony-tails and Armani surplices, sitting around in a minimalist Chapel conversion, drinking Premier Cru communion wine and saying things like:

'Let's run this up the steeple and see who kneels down and prays to it.'

Traditionally, religious advertising consisted of a bit of bell-ringing, a parish newsletter and the times of the main services pinned on the notice-board outside the church, alongside the date of the next bring-and-buy sale. Billy Graham changed all that. But even if the mainstream Church feels it must compete on the spiritual super-highway, does it have to be so crass? 'Surprise! said Jesus to his friends three days after they buried him.' You couldn't make it up. This is straight out of the Cilla Black songbook. Surprise! Surprise! Worra lorra nonsense. How stupid do they think we are? Has it occurred to anyone at a senior level in the Church that ludicrous gimmicks like this are the main reason worshippers are deserting in droves? Most people are perfectly well aware what Easter is all about. They don't have to have it force-fed to them in a manner which would patronise viewers of *Play School*. It is hardly surprising lapsed Christians choose to spend their Sundays cruising the garden centres instead of listening to a vicar called Dave addressing them as if they had a mental age of three. They are sick and tired of trendy clerics banging tambourines, extolling the virtues of international socialism and nuclear disarmament and ringing up the newspapers to proclaim their homosexuality.

It can only be a matter of time before someone in the Churches' Advertising Network tries to rewrite Christmas on the grounds that it discriminates against single mothers. If Labour can modernise Clause Four, the Church can surely be relied upon to do the same for the Ten Commandments, claiming that they are outdated.

If the sign of the cross is laden with irrelevant cultural baggage, what about 'Thou Shalt Not Commit Adultery'? Or the bit about coveting your neighbour's ox? Who do you know who keeps an ox in the back garden these days?

Most people who turn up at church every week do so in the vain hope that their religious leaders will provide them with a constant in their lives. They are looking for someone to reassure them that the values they hold dear still count for something. But the majority of clerics now seem to see themselves as outreach co-ordinators, ministering to welfare scroungers and sexual deviants. Peace, love and understanding translates into anti-Trident marches and lesbian wedding ceremonies. The creed of tolerance has become the creed of proselytising everything which their traditional followers find abhorrent. Very few of them even appear to believe in God any more. They don't understand that it is the 'cultural baggage' which keeps their dwindling congregation trickling through the door. Now they've junked the cross, what will they replace it with – the little red AIDS ribbon?

THE LORD'S PRAYER

– The PC Version

The Church of England has lost the plot completely. In 1994 it voted to remove all references to gender from the Book of Common Prayer. It seems to see God as some kind of employee hired from the jobs page of the *Guardian*. In future the politically correct Lord's Prayer will go something like this:

Our non-specific co-ordinator,
Who art in office on a short-term contract,
Accountable be thy name,
Thy position subject to review,
Thy will according to guidelines laid down by conference,
In sub-committee as in full council.
Give us each day our single person's allowance,
And deliver us artificial insemination on demand.
Forgive us our trespasses and send us on safari,
And lead us not out of the European Union.
For thine is the outreach, the thirty grand and Mondeo,
For ever and ever, until allegations of sexism and
   racial harassment are levelled against you.
Awimmin.

(This prayer welcomes worship from lesbians and gay men,
currently over-represented in the Church of England,

members of ethnic minorities and the physically challenged. This prayer operates a non-smoking policy.)

PORRIDGE

If you're looking for evidence that the country is now run by limp-wristed *Guardian* readers, I suggest you take a glance at the way the prison service is run. Barely a day goes by without yet another story about lax security, of murderers enjoying lobster lunches and rapists being allowed conjugal visits. The standing joke is that prisons are more like country clubs – a theme I developed in a spoof episode of *Porridge*, the old BBC prison comedy, starring Ronnie Barker and the late Richard Beckinsale.

Norman Stanley Fletcher is relaxing in his cell. Enter Godber.

FLETCH: What you doing back so soon, young Godber?

GODBER: I couldn't get near the jacuzzi, Fletch. That team of armed robbers from Bermondsey have been in it all afternoon.

FLETCH: I don't know what this prison's coming to. I can remember when you could just walk into the sauna. Now you have to book.

GODBER: To make matters worse one of the masseurs is off sick. Have you seen Lukewarm today?

FLETCH: Last I heard he was off for a manicure. His boyfriend is coming to stay for the weekend.

GODBER: A word of warning. Genial Harry Grout is on the warpath.

FLETCH: What's upset him, then?

Enter Grout.

GROUT: I am very disappointed, Fletch. Very disappointed indeed. Someone has stolen my Paco Rabanne.

FLETCH: There are a lot of thieves in here, Groutie.

GODBER: Not this afternoon there aren't, Fletch. They're all down the Rat and Ferret watching the football. Our satellite system's on the blink.

GROUT: Have you seen my aftershave, Fletch?

FLETCH: Sorry, Groutie. I'm an Old Spice man myself. Do you want to borrow some?

GROUT: Don't be so common, Fletch. My Dolores is coming to sleep over tonight and she doesn't want to wake up next to someone who smells like a Christmas pudding.

FLETCH: What about the IRA man in D Wing? I saw him in the tailor's earlier on, having his Armani let out. He's expecting a film crew this afternoon.

GODBER: What were you doing in the tailor's?

FLETCH: I'm having to have my trousers let out. I've put so much weight on since I came in here. All that rich food.

GROUT: You should watch that, Lenny. It's why I never eat in the canteen. My personal chef comes in three times a day to make sure I get a balanced diet.

FLETCH: Have you read this speech by Michael Howard?

GODBER: Isn't that the bloke in *Brief Encounter*?

GROUT: Don't be silly, Lenny, you're thinking of Cecil Parkinson.

FLETCH: Celia Johnson.

GROUT: Him, too.

FLETCH: For your information, young Godber, Michael Howard is the Home Secretary. It says here he's going to get tough in the prisons.

GODBER: It's started already, I reckon. That piece of sirloin I had at lunchtime was tough as old boots. Nowhere near as tender as the fillet we had on Tuesday.

FLETCH: The papers are saying Howard has lost control of the prison service and standards are falling.

GROUT: I'd go along with that, Fletch. Have you seen the wine list lately? I can remember when I was in Parkhurst in 1969 they had a very decent cellar. That Roy Jenkins was a great Home Secretary. Nowadays you can't get a decent Barolo in here for love nor money. I have to send out for it.

FLETCH: Speaking of off-licences, didn't your little brother rob one recently, Lenny?

GODBER: That's right, Fletch. And the daft little scrote only went and got himself caught.

FLETCH: What did he get?

GODBER: Two weeks' safari in Africa and a week windsurfing in Barbados.

FLETCH: Did it do him any good?

GODBER: No, Fletch, he got terrible sunburn. His lawyer reckons he's got a good case for suing the social services.

Enter Mr Barraclough.

FLETCH: Fetch us another lager, will you, Mr B?

BARRACLOUGH: Sorry, Fletcher, it all got drunk at the nonses' barbeque last night. I could probably rustle you up a can of Guinness, that's if the IRA inmates haven't had it all. It's their bomb-making class this afternoon.

FLETCH: Silly me, so it is. They had another consignment of Semtex delivered yesterday.

GODBER: Isn't that what they make shirts out of?

FLETCH: That's Aertex.

GROUT: We're still nowhere near recovering my aftershave.

BARRACLOUGH: I thought Lukewarm smelled a bit different today.

GROUT: Someone should remind him that prisons are dangerous places, people get hurt.

GODBER: That's very true, Groutie. Very true indeed. 'Orrible Ives put his back out falling off a stool in the disco.

FLETCH: He's in the hospital wing, in a private ward. Just as well we've all got BUPA these days.

Enter Mr Mackay.

MACKAY: Stand to attention when a senior officer enters, Fletcher.

FLETCH: Do leave off, Mr Mackay. All that went out with the rope. Any more lip and I'll report you to my MP. He's in the next cell.

MACKAY: Where do you think you are, a holiday camp?

GODBER: No, that's where my little brother is. When he got back from windsurfing, he robbed a post office and went ramraiding. So they sent him to Center Parcs.

FLETCH: That'll teach him. The food's nowhere near as good as it is in here. By the way, did you want anything in particular, Mr Mackay?

MACKAY: As a matter of fact, I did, Fletcher. You were due to be released last week.

FLETCH: I was released, Mr Mackay. But I broke back in. Life's much better in here than on the outside.

Far-fetched? Is that what you think? Let me then draw your attention to a report which appeared in the *Daily Mail* on 25 February 1995. It concerned Swaleside prison in Kent, which contains a number of high-security prisoners – including murderer Winston Silcott. It is a prison which has been in the news before, most notably when three officers were suspended after taking a lifer to have dinner with Kenneth Noye, the millionaire villain convicted of handling the proceeds of the notorious Brinks Mat robbery. The prison governor, Ron Tasker, put forward a plan to build a golf course within the prison boundaries at a cost of £40,000 plus VAT. The project was eventually abandoned after the newspapers got wind of it – but not before thousands of pounds had been wasted on golf equipment and commissioning an architect and a landscape gardener.

You really couldn't make it up.

A STEADY RECOVERY

In March, Chancellor Kenneth Clarke conceded that the so-called Feelgood Factor won't return before the next election. Consequently, ministers have been instructed to talk up the economy on every occasion. Mr Clarke himself took the lead at a secret rally of remaining Tory loyalists in a room above a kebab shop in Worksop. Here are the edited highlights of his speech:

> It has become fashionable for the moaning minnies to talk down this government's achievements. The economy is getting stronger all the time. Britain is now the envy of the world. Every day, the evidence of recovery is mounting. For instance, only today a semi-detached house in West Bromwich was sold after just nine months on the market for £16,750 – very close to the asking price of £65,000. A new Spud-U-Like has opened in Jarrow, providing more than two jobs and reversing a sixty-year trend. Sales of paint brushes and Black & Decker Workmates are soaring thanks to this government's policies, which have freed hundreds of thousands of people from employment and given them the incentive to decorate the spare room. Sales of golf clubs and sauna equipment have hit record levels, thanks in the

main to orders placed by Her Majesty's Prison Service. The travel industry is booming. Under the Tories, people who could never have dreamed of a foreign holiday are now spending anything up to six weeks on safari in Africa and windsurfing in Barbados with their social workers.

Britain now has more roadworks, traffic humps, pedestrianisation schemes and one-way systems than any other country in the world, bringing vital orders for the construction and traffic-cone industries. Off-licences, tobacconists, pubs and video-rental stores on sink estates are reporting record business, thanks to our generous welfare provisions for single mothers. Estate agents are enjoying a boom year, letting flats on behalf of the the DSS to unemployed Algerian immigrants and Vietnamese shoplifters. Private dentistry is flourishing. Previously unemployed school-leavers are starting their own businesses, cleaning the windscreens of the record numbers of imported cars being registered in Britain. Other new businesses, selling everything from fake perfume to copies of brand-name jeans and pirate CDs, are springing up on premises which have become vacant because of the long-overdue reorganisation of the banking industry. Britain now has more car boot sales and Oxfam shops than ever before. The security industry is also booming. Britain has more burglar alarms than any other country in the world. Sales of replacement car radios are the highest ever.

It is absurd to suggest that people are worse off under the Tories. Only today I was speaking to a man from Putney, who only five years ago was struggling to get by on an MP's salary of just

£32,000. Today, he has twelve directorships and consultancies, a newspaper column, one radio show and is now in line for another. He's on course to earn £500,000 this year.

Who says Tory policies aren't working?

WHEN THE BOAT COMES IN – FOR GOOD

If you went into a restaurant and ordered egg and chips you wouldn't expect to be handed foie gras and lobster and ordered to eat it at gunpoint. Nor would you expect to be told how to dress and how to hold your knife and fork. And if, instead of a bill for £2.50 for egg and chips, you were presented with a bill for £150 plus VAT for food you hadn't ordered, you'd get up and walk out. You wouldn't expect to be taken to court for non-payment. And you would be horrified to hear prosecuting counsel insist that because you had entered the restaurant of your own free will you were obliged to eat whatever the management decided to serve and pay whatever they decided to charge, regardless of whether you could afford it or not. And you certainly wouldn't accept that, simply because you had gone into a restaurant for egg and chips, the maître d' and chef were entitled to go round to your house, raid your pantry, drink all your booze and sleep with your wife. After taking your credit card and emptying your bank balance. But that is exactly the position in which we now find ourselves in relation to Brussels.

In 1975, the country voted to stay in what was then called the Common Market on the promise of free trade, cheap booze and fags, more jobs and the ability to go on holiday without a passport. And nothing else. Since then the

Common Market has become the European Economic Community, the European Community and now the European Union. The dishes have kept on coming and getting more and more expensive, even though we didn't order them. At no stage have the British people ever been consulted. Instead of a bill for egg and chips we have been presented with a bill for a lobster supper. And the most frightening thing is that our own defence counsel, in this case the British Government, has sided with the prosecution. The line goes: 'You agreed to go in so you have to accept whatever Brussels decides to serve.' The politicians even use the restaurant analogy whenever there are objections to their next grandiose and oppressive scheme. 'You can't have an à la carte Europe.' Why not? The deal was that we entered Chez Europe because of the limited choice Prix Fixe menu in the window.

They lied to us then and they are lying to us still.

To prove my case, I dug out the manifestos of the Pro and Anti lobbies at the time of the 1975 referendum and compared them with what has actually happened. The 'Yes' campaign promised cheaper food, more jobs, net receipts from the community, an export surplus and guaranteed no loss of British sovereignty, cross our hearts and hope to die, stand on me, guv, on my baby's eyes. Yet in virtually every case the 'No' campaigners have been proved right.

Here are some examples of the promises made and broken by the pro-Europeans:

QUOTE: 'If anything the Community has saved us money on food . . . the Common Agricultural Policy now works more flexibly to the benefit of housewives.'

FACT: Average food bills in Britain are £20 a week higher than they would otherwise be if we were allowed to buy food on the world market. This is a direct result of EU membership.

QUOTE: 'It also makes sense to grow more of our own food. That we can do if we stay in the Community . . .'

FACT: Take milk and cheese. Britain could be self-sufficient in dairy products but Europe only allows us to produce 85 per cent of our own needs. Farmers are paid not to grow crops, under the ludicrous set-aside scheme. They are forced to leave 15 per cent of their land idle in exchange for a subsidy of £127 an acre. The Common Agricultural Policy cost was £31 billion in 1994 alone.

QUOTE: The 'Yes' campaign said that Britain would pay a 'fairer share' of the cost of the Community. 'We stand to get back from the market funds of up to £125 million a year.'

FACT: Britain is the second largest contributor, despite a report at the beginning of 1995 which claimed we are among the poorest countries in Europe. A table based on per capita income put Britain sixth. Since we joined we have directly paid £25 billion to Brussels and the actual cost is calculated at ten times that amount.

QUOTE: The 'Yes' campaign said a 'no' vote would mean: 'The immediate effect on trade . . . and hence on jobs . . . could well be disastrous.'

FACT: When we went in we had a healthy trade surplus with Europe. We now have an accumulated trade deficit of £100 billion.

QUOTE: 'There was a threat to employment in Britain from the movement in the Common Market towards economic and monetary union. This could have forced us to accept fixed exchange rates for the pound, restricting industrial growth and so putting jobs at risk. This threat has been removed.'

FACT: That is exactly what happened. Far from the threat being removed, John Major took us into the ERM, resulting in high interest rates, record bankruptcies, record home repossessions, hundreds of thousands of jobs lost. The single currency remains the stated aim of most European governments and a significant number of British politicians, including the Chancellor of the Exchequer, Kenneth Clarke.

QUOTE: 'English Common Law is not affected.'
FACT: English courts are now subordinate to the European Court. If our laws are at variance with European laws, for instance in relation to pregnant ex-servicewomen (*see elsewhere*), British courts can be overruled.

QUOTE: 'No important new policy can be decided in Brussels or anywhere else without the consent of a British minister answerable to a British government and British parliament.'
FACT: Every single working day Brussels spews out new directives, framed by unelected bureaucrats without any reference to parliament.

QUOTE: 'The Community does not mean dull uniformity.'
FACT: The drive towards standardisation throughout Europe is being pursued with a Stalinist zeal, forcing many businesses unable to comply with European directives into bankruptcy. As for 'dull uniformity' Brussels has imposed standards which have eliminated national differences in a whole range of areas. And not only in manufactured goods, either. At the end of 1994, Brussels banned the sale of British acorns because they produce oak trees with bent trunks. European regulations say all oak trees must have straight trunks. You couldn't make this stuff up.

QUOTE: 'Nor will it damage our British traditions and way of life.'
FACT: Where do you want to start? Ask British fishermen if their traditional way of life has not been damaged. The same could be said of family butchers forced to close by absurd and expensive Brussels hygiene regulations and Women's Institutes threatened with prosecution for selling home-made jam without a licence.

What we have been subjected to by most of our leading politicians is a constant stream of lies and deception with regard to our membership of the EU. Just occasionally, one of them breaks ranks and tells the truth. Norman Lamont, the former Chancellor of the Exchequer, says the government has been deliberately deceiving us about Europe. He says there will be a federal Europe and a single currency, because he was there when the deal was done. And he scoffed at Major's ludicrous claims that Britain is 'at the heart of Europe'. In a speech in Bournemouth, Lamont said: 'As a former Chancellor, I cannot pinpoint a single economic advantage that comes to this country as a result of our membership.'

Well, why the hell didn't you tell us sooner, Norm?

Membership of the EU, EC – call it what you like – has cost us £235 billion since 1973 – that's £4000 for every man, woman and child in Britain. Over the next decade our contributions are set to double and we still won't have anything to show for it, except an aircraft-hangar full of regulations, total loss of sovereignty and mass unemployment. The Common Agricultural Policy adds £15 billion a year to our national food bill. For instance, a pound of butter costs 69p within the EU, only 29p outside. Billions are spent paying farmers not to grow anything and plough what they do grow into the ground. There is fraud on a massive scale. Once profitable firms, which provided employment for thousands of British people, are hamstrung by regulations and forced into receivership. Take the case of the glasshouse industry, facing total destruction as a result of new rules on the levels of nitrates in lettuce. This legislation has nothing to do with health and safety, but it has everything to do with screwing Britain. The law has been inspired by Italian and Spanish growers, eager to flood the British market. There is nothing remotely dangerous about the nitrate levels in British lettuces. When did you last hear of someone dying of nitrate poisoning? Exactly. But it is a fact that lettuces grown under glass have higher nitrate levels than those grown in the open air. And in Britain, because of our climate, most lettuces are grown under glass.

In Italy and Spain – well, I never – they grow their lettuces in the open. So once we have smashed our home-grown glasshouse industry on the orders of Europe, we will have to buy Italian and Spanish lettuces at whatever price they decide to charge us for them.

Politicians of all parties know the truth about Europe, but they are like rabbits caught in the Brussels headlights. With one or two honourable exceptions they go along with this madness. I am convinced that the only way out is to withdraw completely from the Community and then renegotiate a new deal based on free trade. The politicians say this is unworkable and try to scare us with dire warnings of bankruptcies, unemployment and ruin. What the hell do they think we've got already? The truth of the matter is that there is a whole world out there willing to trade with Britain, especially across the Atlantic, in the Commonwealth and the Pacific Rim. And as for Europe refusing to trade with us, that's absolute nonsense. We are one of the richest markets in Europe. They are desperate to sell their goods to us. In which case, they can do so on our terms. We want a free-trade deal and can do without the fancy, expensive extras.

Egg and chips please. And only egg and chips.

Such benefits as we were promised – cheap booze and fags – have failed to materialise. Our Government is determined that we will not even be thrown this scrap of comfort. Despite the introduction of the single market which was meant to harmonise duties throughout Europe, British duties have not been cut. Alcohol duties on Continental Europe are a fraction of those in Britain. Scotch bought in France is half the price of Scotch bought in Scotland. Shepherd Neame beer, brewed in Kent, can be bought for a third of the price in France. Is it any wonder pubs and off-licences close to the Channel ports are closing?

If you want to pay a sensible price for your booze you still have to go through the ridiculous charade of travelling across the Channel to buy it. Cross-Channel ferries groan under the weight of cut-price grog. One entrepreneur from Essex has even set up stall on the Calais ringroad to serve those who can't wait the extra kilometre to the Mammouth Hypermarche.

The predictable British response to the European free-trade initiative has been to send teams of customs officers to raid restaurants, off-licences and pubs to make sure that drink bought for alleged personal consumption is not being re-sold. Kent police began stopping cars, coaches and lorries to check that loads are not excessive. (Oh, and by the way, would you mind blowing into this, sir?) All this nonsense could be avoided if our taxes were cut to European levels. No chance. Britain is run on the principle that if something costs more in Europe then our prices have to go up to bring us into line. But if something is more expensive here, it stays more expensive. The Government will play 'good Europeans' and obey the rules when it comes to destroying the fishing industry in the name of quotas and shutting down abattoirs and cheese shops which fail to meet operating-theatre hygiene standards. But a few bob off a bottle of lager? You must be joking.

Whenever I cross swords with rampant pro-Europeans like Hugh Dykes on TV and challenge them to name a single, tangible benefit which has arisen from our EC membership they bluff and bluster and yell 'Little Englander'. The best they can come up with is that there hasn't been another European war. True, but that's got nothing to do with Brussels, it has everything to do with NATO and the strong American influence. And when they claim that there hasn't been a European war, what on earth do they think has been going on in the former Yugoslavia for the past three years or so? What is going on in the former Soviet Union? We must look eastwards if we want to discover what will eventually happen in the EU. The great European adventure will end in tears, if it doesn't end in blood. As the former Eastern Bloc countries are demonstrating, you can't force people to conform to an homogeneous norm. You can't have British fish shops run from Strasbourg, or Spanish commissioners deciding whether or not Scottish housewives are allowed to make their own butterscotch for sale at church fêtes. More to the point, you can't have German bankers setting British monetary policy or French generals deciding British defence policy. My fear, indeed my prediction, is that unless someone calls a halt, then the whole affair will end in blood. I can envisage a future European superstate wracked by terrorism from separatist groups – Basques, Danes, Bretons, even Bavarians, and especially Britons. One thing nationalists have learned from the IRA is that you can bomb and murder your way to a political end. British nationalists are capable of absorbing that lesson and there are a lot of disillusioned, disaffected ex-servicemen on the dole who would make willing recruits. Unless the politicians wake up, the initiative will be seized from them. Unless the British people are offered a real choice over Europe then it will end violently. Where there is no democracy, democrats take to the streets. And when they are forced off the streets, they crawl underground, and start making bombs.

This is not what we ordered. Egg and chips would have done nicely, thank you.

It is a scandal that successive British governments have surrendered our traditional fishing grounds to foreigners. The French don't allow us to harvest their grapes. Spanish orange groves are not a 'common resource'. So why should they be given free access to British fish? The quotas allocated to British fishermen by Brussels are risible – and shrinking. Imagine the frustration of our fishermen as they are forcibly tied up in port and have to sit and watch foreign vessels plundering out waters with the full backing of the British Government. Whereas the Spanish have a handful of fisheries inspectors, all based in Madrid, the British coast is crawling with men from the ministry enforcing rules to the last dot and comma. And whereas the French navy sails in support of French fishermen, the British Navy turns its might against British fishermen. Instead of threatening rogue Spanish boats, our Navy arrests British skippers when push comes to shove in disputed waters. God knows what the members of the Royal Navy, heirs to a tradition embracing Nelson and Trafalgar, feel about having to carry out these orders from the politicians.

> I joined the Navy to see the sea.
> And what did I do?
> I ended up arresting British fishermen for
> defending their waters against the Spanish.

Er, doesn't quite have the same ring to it, does it?

Perhaps more than any single issue, fishing graphically illustrates the way our sovereignty has been surrendered and we have been subjugated to foreign interests by stupid and venal politicians because of fear of missing the European gravy train. This all began when Grocer Heath decided to declare British fishery grounds a common resource in his desperation to bribe his way into the Common Market. It soon became apparent that there wasn't enough fish to go round. Surprise, surprise. So quotas were introduced to prevent over-fishing, forcing thousands of trawler men out of business. The British

Government – determined to be seen to be 'good Europeans' – sent teams of Ministry officials to the ports to make sure our fishermen played by the rules. The rest of the EU took little notice of the regulations. When the French government tried to enforce the quotas, their fishermen rioted, attacked imports and British vessels – just as the French farmers had burned our lamb lorries. The French government – displaying its usual spine – backed down. The British fishing fleet has been destroyed by a Common Fisheries Policy which was not even enforceable in law until the Maastricht Treaty was forced through parliament. It came to a head at the end of 1994 when the so-called Irish Box waters were opened to Spanish vessels. Spain's mechanised trawlers were officially given free access to hoover up British fish. The government made it an issue of confidence. Major had given his word to his foreign chums, so the people who he is paid to represent could get stuffed. Consequently 90 per cent of the fish caught off Newlyn, in Cornwall, now ends up on the dining tables of Madrid. The government then spent £28 million of British taxpayers' money paying British fishermen to burn their own boats – 'decommission' them in Brussels-speak. It was hardly necessary. Foreign boats have been plundering British and Irish waters – which account for 80 per cent of Europe's fish stocks – ever since the Treaty of Accession was drawn up in 1972. Much of the fishing has been illegal, but Britain has been too weak or too compliant to do anything about it. If anyone had said twenty years ago that a British government would one day send British naval vessels to arrest British fishermen protesting against a British government decision to hand over British fishing grounds to Spanish trawlers, they'd have been laughed out of court.

You couldn't make it up.

British fishermen could not have been blamed if they had

taken a leaf out of the French book and blockaded ports, prevented ships and lorries unloading and sabotaged catches of imported fish. It would have been violence born of frustration, not just with recent events but with two decades of destruction of their industry. But fishermen, like everyone else, have become browbeaten, disillusioned and resigned to their fate after two decades of betrayal by a government which always talks tough and carries a small stick into negotiations in Brussels. It reserves the big stick for beating the British. You wouldn't have believed that a great maritime nation would ever have ended up like this. What would have happened, for instance, to 'When The Boat Comes In'?

You can't have a fishy
On a little dishy
You can't have a fishy
'Cos the boat's been burned.

You can't have a haddock
You can't have a bloater
And as for Britain's quota
That has gone to Spain.

Dance to the Spanish
Sing for your supper
Eat bread and butter
'Cos the boat's been burned.

You can't have yer mussels
They've been sent to Brussels
You can't have a mackerel
'Cos the boat's been burned.

(*Traditional*)

WHO DO YOU THINK YOU ARE KIDDING?

To commemorate the fiftieth anniversary of D-Day, I discovered the BBC had commissioned a special edition of *Dad's Army*, which has never been shown. The leading roles were all to have been taken by present-day politicians. In keeping with BBC policy, the script was updated to embrace current attitudes towards Europe, in line with Brussels directive 6/6/44.

THE CAST

Capt Mainwaring	John Major
Sgt Wilson	Douglas Hurd
Cpl Jones	Bill Cash
Pte Pike	Michael Portillo
Pte Walker	Michael Heseltine
The Vicar	John Gummer
Mrs Pike	Virginia Bottomley
Pte Godfrey	Lord Whitelaw
Pte Fraser	Malcolm Rifkind

The scene is the church hall, Walmington-on-Sea. Enter Cpl Jones.

JONES: Don't panic! It's D-Day. Don't panic!

MAINWARING: Pull yourself together, Jones. What's the matter?

JONES: It's D-Day, Mr Mainwaring, sir. We are invading Europe.

WILSON: I do wish you wouldn't use such emotive language, Jonesey. We are not invading Europe, as such. We are going to put ourselves at the heart of Europe.

MAINWARING: At the heart of a multi-speed Europe, if you don't mind, Wilson.

WILSON: I really am so sorry, sir. How silly of me.

JONES: I wish I was going too, sir. Them Jerries don't like it up 'em, Mr Mainwaring, sir.

MAINWARING: Jones, I've told you before, there is no room for Euro-scepticism in this platoon. Any more of that and you'll find yourself on trial for war crimes.

PIKE: My mum says the only good German is a dead German. That's what John Mills told David Niven in that film we saw at the Rialto the other night. Isn't that right, Uncle Arthur?

WILSON: Do be quiet, Frank.

MAINWARING: Those are the kind of attitudes which got us in this mess in the first place. If only we had stuck to the Munich treaty, none of this would have happened.

Enter Walker.

WALKER: Sorry I'm late, I had a bit of business to attend to.

MAINWARING: Don't you know there's a war on, Walker?

WALKER: Of course, I've just seen all the planes going overhead on their way to Germany.

JONES: That'll teach Jerry. Go on, my brave boys. Good old Bomber Harris.

MAINWARING: I'm warning you, Jones.

WALKER: We seem to have earned very well out of the deal.

WILSON: What deal?

WALKER: For the planes. Spitfies, Hurricanes, Wellingtons, Lancasters. My mate at the War Office flogged the lot to the Germans.

PIKE: But we built those planes. We shouldn't be selling them to our enemy.

MAINWARING: Stupid boy. That's no way to talk about our European partners. Germany must be free to invest in Britain, just as we must be free to invest in Germany. And anyway, we've still got Rover.

PIKE: But they keep trying to kill us, Mr Mainwaring. They keep dropping bombs on us. And they've invaded Poland. And France. And the Low Countries, wherever they are.

WILSON: Oh, do shut up, Frank.

PIKE: Don't you tell me to shut up or I'm telling my mum.

MAINWARING: For your information, Pike, Germany did not invade Poland or anywhere else for that matter. Herr Hitler has merely been carrying out a policy of enlarging the Community and moving towards political and monetary union.

WALKER: I'm all in favour of a single currency, provided it's in cash. Anyone want to buy any cigarettes?

PIKE: My mum says people shouldn't be allowed to smoke.

WALKER: She should try telling Winston Churchill. I've just sold him 200 Havanas.

Enter the Vicar.

VICAR: Are you going to be much longer?

MAINWARING: What do you want?

VICAR: Don't you talk to me in that tone of voice, this is my church hall. And as from tomorrow I am converting it to a Roman Catholic church hall, to bring us into line with the rest of Europe.

MAINWARING: Get him out of here, Jones.

JONES: Right, sir. Yes, sir. *(Fixing bayonet)* Left, right, left, right.

VICAR: You'll be hearing from the Pope about this.

WILSON: Well done, Jonesey. By the way, did you bring my half pound of sausages?

JONES: I'm sorry, Mr Wilson. But the man from the Ministry came and closed my shop down yesterday. He said under new directives my premises were unhygienic, my sausages didn't comply with European standards and I was being prosecuted for not using metric measures.

PIKE: My mum isn't going to be very happy. She looks forward to her sausage at the weekends, doesn't she, Uncle Arthur?

WILSON: Be quiet, Frank.

WALKER: I know where I might be able to lay my hands on some sausages, if you don't mind a bit of garlic on them. I'm taking the van over as part of the D-Day invasion and picking up a load of cheap booze in Calais. I could liberate a few kilos of German sausages while I'm there.

JONES: You be careful, Joe. You might get hurt. Make sure you don't trip over any towels on the beach.

GODFREY: My sister Dolly had some German sausages once. They didn't agree with her at all.

MAINWARING: Now pay attention, men. I want no more of this defeatist talk. I know the casualties are going to be heavy this week . . .

Voice off.

MRS PIKE: Frank, Frank. Are you in there, Frank?

WILSON: Oh dear.

MAINWARING: What's the meaning of this?

PIKE: Now you're for it. My mum says if you think I'm following you into Europe, you must be joking. You're going to get slaughtered, you are. Just like you did at the local elections.

MAINWARING: Stupid boy.

JONES: Don't panic. Don't panic.

FRASER: We're all doomed.

EU-POSITIVE

Tory Euro-fanatics have grouped together under the banner 'Positive Europeans'. It makes them sound as if they've got some terrible disease. Which they probably have. What other explanation can there be for the Gadarene rush towards a European superstate? Perhaps we should start treating it as an illness. It might help us understand the eagerness of politicians to sell our souls to Brussels. Then we might see stories like this appearing in the newspapers:

> Fears were growing last night for the former Prime Minister Sir Edward Heath. Sir Edward, who was diagnosed EEC-positive many years ago, is believed to have developed full-blown federalism. He is said to be beyond hope. A number of other leading politicians have also contracted the disease. They include Sir Leon Brittan, Lord Jenkins, Lord Howe and the Chancellor, Kenneth Clarke. The virus passes through a number of stages –known in the medical profession as EEC, EC, ERM, EMU and EU – before the patient contracts full- blown federalism. Victims put on an enormous amount of weight, suffer serious delusions of grandeur and start speaking in a ridiculous voice. They behave irrationally and crave approval from foreigners,

often at the expense of their own country. Over the past twenty-four years, the victims have given away billions of pounds to corrupt farmers in France, Italy and Greece and handed over the bulk of Britain's fish stocks to the Spanish. They develop a paranoia about hygiene, demanding absurd regulations governing butchers' shops and attacking Women's Institutes for using wooden breadboards.

The disease spread rapidly through the Brussels restaurant scene – the political equivalent of the San Francisco bath-house scene. One sufferer said: 'We didn't know what we were doing then. We never took any precautions. We never imagined it would end like this. We should have known there was no such thing as a free lunch.' A number of young men who came into contact with Sir Edward in the 1970s, including the Foreign Secretary, Douglas Hurd, are also believed to be infected. And doctors are increasingly worried about Prime Minister John Major. One said: 'He hasn't put on all that much weight yet, but he is exhibiting some of the classic symptoms – the funny voice, the delusions of grandeur and the urge to give away British sovereignty.' Successive governments have ignored the problem, hoping it will go away. But the truth is that we are all at risk.

Complete withdrawal is the only safe solution. Just say No.

LITTLEJOHN'S LAW OF LOCAL GOVERNMENT

Littlejohn's Law of Local Government states that the bigger the council and the bigger the budget, the worse the services. That is, what we consider to be services, anyway – housing, education, transport, public cleaning, libraries. Not 'services' as defined by most councils – armies of outreach co-ordinators for sexual deviants, the promotion of racial division and millions of little red bricks. As I'm writing this chapter, the London Borough of Haringey is digging up all the pavements near my house and relaying them with fancy zig-zag patterned ornamental bricks, which look absolutely hideous. No one asked them to do this. There wasn't much wrong with the pavements as they were, certainly nothing that a bit of levelling and a few bags of cement couldn't have sorted out. It's the second time they've dug up the pavement recently. The first time was outside the public toilets which have been closed for a few years because of 'lack of resources'. (What 'resources' do you need to keep a toilet open, apart from the occasional visit by a cleaner, a change of bog roll and the Old Bill dropping in on a regular basis to move on the shirtlifters who have decided to used the place as a singles bar?)

On this occasion the pavement was being dug up to install a new £150,000 bus information system. So now passengers know that they have got to wait twenty-two minutes for the next bus in the freezing cold rather than wondering if they will ever see a bus again. If they'd have asked the poor sods at the bus stop what their priorities were, they'd probably have said: (1) more buses; and (2) reopen the toilet, in case we get caught short waiting hours for the next bus to come along. But then no one ever asks the public what they want. Local government is about gimmickry and political correctness. By rights, Haringey shouldn't be allowed to spend anything on pavements, except for essential repairs. At the last count, Haringey's debt was £561 million, bigger than the national debts of countries like Haiti and Malta.

I've spent years banging on about waste, inefficiency and political lunacy. People told me it was only confined to the barmier London boroughs. So I travelled to Peterborough, where I cut my teeth as a reporter twenty-four years ago, covering the Town Hall in the days before local government reorganisation. Even then, I should have realised the way things were going. I can recall the council leader trying to lend Peterborough United FC £100,000 of ratepayers' money to buy the Bermudan centre forward Clyde Best from West Ham. Things are different now, I was told. This is a model, moderate Labour council. So I decided to investigate.

Perhaps the most graphic illustration of inefficiency was the dog-catching service, which was costing £89,700 a year – of which £27,000 was swallowed up by Town Hall bureaucracy, or 'cost of democracy' as the council quaintly called it. It worked out that it cost £184 to catch every dog! The council had also decided that it needed an Olympic swimming pool to attract world-class competition to the city. Unfortunately the pool was built one metre short. Result, no competition and everyone using the pool had to be subsidised to the tune of £5 a head. So the council decided to close it. Even then it cost £85,000 a year just to keep shut. Peterborough also built a community centre at a cost of £2 million. It costs £125,000 a year to run. It was supposed to be for the benefit of everyone, but Muslim extremists threatened to burn it to the ground if a drop of alcohol was allowed on the premises. Result: the community centre was handed over to the Muslims. Women have to enter round the back and stay in a separate room. This is allowed to go on despite the tens of thousands of pounds Peterborough spends on extending 'women's rights'. Perhaps the finest example of local government incompetence was the council-run Peterborough Lottery, which pre-dated the National Lottery by some years. In 1992, the lottery made a loss of £5385. That's right, a loss. Whoever heard of anyone making a loss on a lottery? An auditor's report concluded that the cost of administering the lottery so exceeded the income that it should be closed down. The council voted to keep it going for at least another two years.

We keep being told that this kind of lunacy is all in the past. Utter nonsense. The local government party is still in full swing (see chapter on Town Hall jobs for further details). After writing about the madness in the Town Halls for many years, I was delighted when a former Labour Party adviser, Leo McKinstry, jumped ship and confirmed everything I had ever written – and more. McKinstry, a former Labour councillor in Islington, defected to the right-wing *Spectator* with tales of waste and excess. He said the final straw was an industrial tribunal in which a transvestite council worker was suing neighbouring Hackney, another Labour authority, because he had been barred from wearing a skirt to work – all being paid for by the taxpayer. You really couldn't make this stuff up. He described Labour's record in local government as 'a mean-minded cocktail of political correctness, intervention and abuse of public money'. In Islington, the council was so inefficient and plagued by restrictive practices that when the staff went on strike the council tax collection rate actually improved. He quoted a barrister's report on Islington council, which said the cash office was staffed by the innumerate, the filing done by the disorganised and the reception desk staffed by the surly and charmless. At any one time, 6 per cent of Islington employees were on sick leave, costing £11 million a year. And this isn't only confined to London. Humberside owes £180 million, nearly as much as Mongolia, and runs an ice-hockey team which loses £75,000 a year. In Liverpool, the council owes £774 million, more than Mauritius, yet still found the money to spend £12,000 on demonstrations against Christopher Columbus. Honest.

Birmingham, once a proud model of municipal efficiency, owes a staggering £1367 million, three times more than Albania owed after forty years of communism. I suppose when you owe that kind of money, £100,000 for an annual festival to bring together disabled lesbians is a mere bagatelle. Birmingham also sent its former leader, Sir Richard Knowles, to oversee the South African elections at a cost of £3000. That must have been a great comfort to Nelson Mandela and Chief Buthelezi. You can start the voting now, chaps, the Mayor of Birmingham's arrived. What the conduct of the South African elections has got to do with Birmingham City Council is a mystery. I am sure council tax-payers in the West Midlands could think of better ways of spending three grand. This is not the first time Brum has behaved like an arm of the Foreign Office. In December, a councillor flew to Cairo to 'enable Birmingham to make a significant contribution to the consolidation of the peace process in the Middle East'. And don't forget the duty-frees. During ten years in power,

Birmingham's Labour group has sent delegations to Brunei, Sierra Leone, Puerto Rico, Malaysia, Borneo, Thailand, Zambia and Malawi. Heavens knows what all this madness cost. Last year alone, Brum spent £90,000 on foreign travel for councillors and officers. Meanwhile the city still has some of the worst housing conditions in Europe. A small fortune also went on an abortive bid to bring the Olympics to Birmingham (which stood as little chance as that of Manchester, discussed in a separate chapter). Even the presence of 100 Brummie councillors, officials and their wives at a knees–up in Lausanne failed to persuade the IOC that Balsall Heath was a more tantalising venue than Barcelona.

Local government in Britain is a monster out of control. Councillors are elected to mend the roads, make sure the pavements are swept and the public libraries and lavatories are maintained. They are not there to play at international statesmen. Nor are they there to enforce their warped notions of political correctness by mounting anti–nuclear, anti–smoking and anti–fox–hunting campaigns. It is a pity that party politics play any part in local government. Town Halls were always better run by ratepayers' candidates and independents. We need a revival of the tradition if the local government juggernaut is ever to be brought under control. Once when I wrote about the latest piece of lunacy in Haringey I received an angry letter from the director of public relations. I subsequently discovered that at the same time Haringey was closing toilets and playgroups the public relations budget had risen to something in the order of £400,000 to campaign against government 'cuts'. When I started covering local government, the council didn't even have a press officer. But there was always a toilet open when you needed one. But in today's brave new world, public relations always comes before public conveniences.

ONLY THE 'UNQUALIFIED' AND 'MENTALLY CHALLENGED' NEED APPLY

Most of the madness in Britain has been imported from the United States. Nowhere is this more apparent than in government recruiting offices, where the high priests of political correctness hold sway. And if you think it can't get any more crazy, then you are wrong. Already it is impossible to get work in the health service or with local authorities unless you are a non-smoking, disabled, ethnic lesbian. In America, even if you meet those strict criteria, it is still not enough. There is no minority too small, no disability too rare. In fact, in some cases employers seem to be advertising exclusively for those who are uniquely unqualified for the job. For instance, in 1994, the US Fish and Wildlife Service advertised a job vacancy with the specification that the 'mentally challenged are strongly urged to apply'.

You couldn't make it up, you really couldn't.

I wonder what was going through the minds of whoever placed the advertisement. What exactly did they mean by mentally challenged? Did they mean those with learning difficulties? Or the criminally insane? The traditional response to the employment needs of the mentally challenged has been to hand them a broom and stick them in a corner out of harm's way. That way everybody's happy. The educationally subnormal get a useful role in life, the floors get swept and the rest of us salve our consciences secure in the knowledge that we've done something for the less fortunate. But in America, that is no longer good enough. The mentally challenged have the same rights as everyone else. Which is, presumably, how Al Gore got to become Vice President.

I'm all for finding work for the simple, but I don't want them in charge of my bank account or running the fire service. But the logical conclusion of the American initiative is that refusing to employ one of the mentally challenged as a bomber pilot or professor of higher mathematics will pretty soon amount to discrimination. As will failure to employ anyone who wants a job, regardless of whether or not they have the ability to do it. If you think I'm joking, consider another US job advertisement, from the Forestry Service, which announced that 'Only unqualified applicants will be considered'.

So there you have it. You can work hard at school, go on to University and still find yourself passed over for a job you have trained all your life for in favour of a half-wit who has played truant and sat in front of the TV picking his nose and who can't even spell his own name. In fact, in this case, it will be a positive advantage to be illiterate and innumerate. And take my word for it, it will happen here soon.

The one thing you will notice is that these advertisements, on both sides of the Atlantic, only ever appear for jobs in the public sector. You never find the IBMs of this world advertising for mentally challenged, unqualified candidates to work on their latest micro-processor technology. That's because the private sector is driven by profit and innovation. It can't afford to carry passengers. The public sector couldn't give a stuff. It is a monopoly provider, funded by unlimited supplies of taxpayers' money confiscated on pain of imprisonment. It can afford this lunacy, because its 'customers' can't go elsewhere and can't refuse to cough up. Fifteen years of allegedly radical Conservative government, elected on a promise to hack back the role of the state and cut public spending, has presided over the exact opposite. If you doubt what I am saying, pick up the *Guardian* jobs supplement any Wednesday. There are regularly more than twenty pages of adverts for public sector appointments. There follows a selection, taken from two issues at random.

They are the usual assortment of Afro-Caribbean / sexual equality / social work / outreach / development / AIDS / project / team leader / drugs / alcohol / liaison / support / welfare rights / immigration appeals / emotionally disturbed / re-source / community / co-ordinator / analyst / multi-racial / activities / non-sexist / black women's refuge / disabilities / counsellors / professionals. East London and The City Health Authority, for instance, urgently sought an Afro-Caribbean or African Health Promotion Officer to run a Hypertension Reduction Scheme in Hackney. Salary starting at £16,485. North West Surrey Health Authority created the post of Clinical Audit Co-ordinator to conduct a 'uni-professional and multidisciplinary' audit across 'residential and community components'. If you understood what all that meant, fifteen grand could have been yours. Bart's Hospital, in London, under threat of closure and complaining about under-funding, managed to come up with £16,683 to attract a new female HIV counsellor and a further £18,700 for someone to 'assess the range of social, nursing and support needs of clients'. Aberdeen Drugs Action – which boasts that it consists of a co-ordinator, 1.5 project workers (one of them must be vertically challenged), two outreach workers, an HIV/drugs worker, a needle exchange worker, an administrator, a secretary and a part-time cleaner – wanted to hire a rural worker, presumably to combat the crack epidemic among Scottish farmers. Waltham Forest social services department wanted a new publicity and information worker for its HIV unit. The tens of millions of pounds already spent by the Government on AIDS education obviously didn't get through to some people in North East London.

Westminster – supposedly a flagship Tory council – wanted a male Afro-Caribbean project worker, £22,323 a year and a benefit package including free swimming facilities. If the Notting Hill carnival is anything to go by, Afro-Caribbeans are quite capable of organising things themselves. Sheffield Council had £19,656 to spend on a co-ordinator to beef up the staff reporting to the Strategic I Manager at the Pakistan Enterprise Centre. Why? Pakistanis are among the most enterprising people in the world. The banana republic of Lambeth – technically bankrupt – was still able to find twenty-nine grand to spend on a new Head of Equalities Unit.

Among the real jewels on offer was the £70,000 a year being offered by Merton, in South London, for a new Social Services Director. That's as much as the Prime Minister gets. Thamesdown – which is what Swindon calls itself these days – was desperate to pay someone sixteen grand a year to become a Play Development Officer. 'The successful candidate will need to be a well-organised self-starter and effective communicator and be able to demonstrate an empathy with children and have a commitment to improving equality of opportunity.' In my experience, children are quite capable of playing happily without any professional help. It is stopping them which often proves difficult. Why they should need special guidance from a full-time NALGO member is beyond me. Does 'The Farmer's In His

Den' now have to conform to EU regulations under the Common Agricultural Policy? Perhaps 'Cowboys and Indians' is to be outlawed on the grounds that it discriminates against Native Americans. Thamesdown is keen on doling out taxpayers' money. It also advertised for a £14,000 a year Citizen Advocacy Development Worker and a team of stress counsellors to help children get in touch with their feelings.

In Leicester, the Highfields Workshop announced it was changing its name to the Imani Ujima Centre and as a result urgently needed to hire 'dynamic, self-motivated and creative people who can undertake the challenging roles to provide resources, activities and services to meet the needs and demands of the local African Caribbean Community'. Like all such schemes, this is patronising nonsense. It implies that Afro-Caribbeans are too stupid to do anything for themselves. But this is a job creation exercise, plain and simple. Apart from all the money being spent on the 'extensive refurbishment' involved in turning the Highfields Workshops into the Imani Ujima Centre, it put another bunch of *Guardian* readers on the payroll at up to twenty grand each.

One morning I decided to amuse myself by adding up the salaries of all the staff being sought in the *Guardian* public appointments page. That day there were thirty-seven pages of positions and it took me more than forty-five minutes. The total bill came to £7,602,385 – not including the cost of all the cars, pensions, sports clubs, brass door plates, computers, secretaries and sick pay. Multiply that by fifty-two and you get a pretty accurate picture of how much it costs the British taxpayer to recruit staff for Town Halls every year. It came to £395,324,020 – give or take the odd £500,000 here and there, depending on how many Eritrean lesbians Stockport council finds itself short of from week to week. And bear in mind that these are by and large new positions, created to meet 'needs' identified by the 'caring professions' and to comply with hastily thought-out and ill-conceived legislation spewing out by the stomach-full from Westminster and Brussels. It is merely the tip of an iceberg of titanic proportions and explains why a Conservative government found itself borrowing money at the rate of £1 billion a week and raising taxes. Interestingly, you never see any of these jobs advertised in the *Sun*, the *Daily Mail* or the *Daily Telegraph*. Never mind welcoming applications from gay/lesbian/ethnic minority/candidates and disabilities. What they really mean is: Lefties Only Need Apply. After fourteen years of Tory government, Town Halls are all run by Labour-voting *Guardian* readers – regardless of who controls the council. Which is why spending goes up.

The long march through the institutions which began in the sixties is almost complete, but shows no sign of running out of steam. Nor will it while politicians fail to grasp the scale of the problem. Michael Portillo is supposed to be one of the most right-wing Conservative members of the Cabinet. Yet when he was questioned by David Frost in January 1995, he said the big problem which all politicians worried about was whether or not the wealth-creating sector – i.e. private industry and the taxpayer – could afford to continue to support the wealth-consuming sector. If all he is concerned about is affordability and not desirability, then it means we are in deep trouble. Because it assumes that all of the so-called 'services' we pay for are vital. Which is how we end up with bearded clowns on twenty-five grand a year telling kids how to play cowboys and Indians and lesbians trawling council refuse depots tearing down Page Three calendars at the taxpayers' expense and filling libraries with homosexual propaganda. Pretty soon, councils will be following the American lead and advertising for 'unqualified' and 'mentally challenged' candidates to work in the finance department. And when that day comes, the lunatics really will have taken over the asylum.

But what chance is there of local government being cut down to size if national government goes on expanding? What is needed is an immediate freeze on all recruitment in the public sector. I realised, however, that there was little chance of this happening when it was revealed that the Chancellor, Kenneth Clarke, was hiring yet another over-paid management consultant at a cost of £2000 a day. Miss Wendy Pritchard was brought in to tell Treasury officials how to 'relate' to each other. It is said that this will make the Treasury operate more efficiently. I could have saved Mr Clarke some money. In fact, I'd have been willing to offer my services for nothing. The simple way to make the Treasury run more efficiently would be to sack at least half the people who work there as a basis for negotiation. Having done that, I would then go on to close down most government departments. They are all largely superfluous, their only role to provide employment for the people who work in them. Most of the business of government just gets in the way.

We could quite happily live without the Department of Trade and Industry and the Ministry of Agriculture, for instance. When Britain accounted for a quarter of the world's exports, we managed to get by quite happily with a simple Board of Trade. Now there are thousands upon thousands of bureaucrats making a bloody nuisance of themselves without helping sell a single washer overseas. When I started out as industrial correspondent the DTI was responsible for most of the nationalised industries – steel, gas, electricity, British Leyland and so on. But since the Thatcher revolution all those industries have been sold off, become profitable private concerns and shed thousands upon thousands of jobs to become more efficient. The DTI, however, still continues to employ just as many people as it did in 1979. What on earth do they find to do all day?

When we were self-sufficient in food and fish, the Min of Ag had a few dozen officials making sure that sheep were dipped properly. Today we have legions of inspectors and administrators – whose sole job seems to be to harass farmers, shut down abattoirs and put fishermen out of business on the orders of Brussels – and food imports have reached record levels. For that matter, what the hell does the Department of the Environment do for a living? And why does it need 6687 employees to do it? The Ministry of Defence has more civil servants than soldiers. But instead of contracting, it has also been expanding. Even though it doesn't have to procure so many uniforms, tanks and weapons, it still managed to spend £100 million procuring a new procurement centre near Bristol. This 100-acre site houses 5500 bureaucrats, a lakeside panorama and superb sports facilities.

In total, the number of civil servants employed by Whitehall has increased under John Major to 565,000. The civil service in 1994 cost £12 billion a year in wages alone, not including the quangos and semi-autonomous bodies paid for out of our taxes. So it's hardly surprising that ministers don't seem to give a stuff about the money wasted by local councils, Government agencies and the NHS. What's one more management consultant at the Treasury when the number of managers employed in the health service rose from 510 to 13,500 in the five years to 1994. It wouldn't be so bad if we were getting any better services. But we're not. Quite the opposite in many cases. Government officials spend their entire lives dreaming up new ways to obstruct and inconvenience us. The new legions of managers and consultants are lining their pockets at the expense of front-line staff and the paying public. Their idea of saving money is sacking soldiers, nurses, porters, road sweepers, teachers — while at the same time building themselves vast new office complexes and treating each other to M-reg Scorpios. We hear a lot about wards and schools being closed, but when was the last time you read of a cutback in the number of offices and photocopiers?

The jamboree goes on and on. At a time when the operation of the NHS has come in for more criticism than ever before and wards and hospitals are being closed for so-called lack of resources, the health service management decided to treat itself to a brand-new office complex in Leeds, costing £55 million, complete with swimming pool, hand-woven carpets and computer-controlled waterfalls. I don't suppose staff there need any expensive help 'relating' to each other. It's more likely to prove difficult stopping them relating like rabbits. Against this kind of background, the appointment of a £2000-a-day consultant at the Treasury doesn't even amount to a round of drinks. Still, it's only money. Our money. And the government doesn't look on our money in the same way we do.

Imagine for a moment that you are heavily overdrawn. Your bank manager tells you to make economies or else. The causes are obvious. You've run up your credit cards to the limit, lost a fortune on the gee-gees and owe more on the mortgage than your house is worth. You run three cars and take two foreign holidays a year, always flying First Class. The kids are at private schools, you've got gold card accounts at every department store in town. You live on fillet steak and champagne at home and eat out at expensive restaurants when the pubs close at night. But you haven't paid the gas and electric bills and the council tax demand has just crash-landed on the doormat. The HP on the dishwasher is due and you're six months behind on the TV rental. Is it any wonder that NatWest won't give you another loan and your application for a Bank of Venezuela VISA card has been turned down? And, to make matters worse, the missus wants another baby, even though you've got six children already. The bank manager spells out the stark alternatives – either make serious economies immediately or you will make a great court case. You don't have to be the Chief Secretary to the Treasury to work out that your present lifestyle can't be maintained on a bus conductor's wages. All is not lost. There are a couple of options: You can sell the house and move to a smaller one in a less expensive area. You can sell the Range Rover, the Jag and the Ferrari and buy a secondhand Sierra Estate. You can cut up the credit cards, stop gambling, stop going to the pub every night, stop eating out, start living on mince and carrots and baked beans and soggy toast, take a week at Skegness in June instead of a month in Barbados twice a year, send back the video, send the kids to state schools and tell the wife you are having a vasectomy. If you're lucky, you might just clear off all your debts and the bank manager will put you back on the Christmas card list. In a couple of years he might even consider giving you a modest loan. All that you could work out in five minutes on the back of a beer mat. Alternatively you can put off the fateful day by calling in a consultant to review your finances and suggest savings. He knows you're not really serious, otherwise he wouldn't be there. So he spends six weeks going through your drawers and your bank statements and looking at your grocery bill. Eventually he presents you with a report. He recommends buying jumbo freezer packs of sirloin steak instead of fresh fillet and own-brand champagne instead of vintage Bollinger. If you must go to the pub, he says, try to stay on singles. As for holidays, he suggests flying Club

Class instead of First. And trading in the Range Rover for a Mitsubishi Shogun. All this will save you around £5000 a year. Then he presents you with his bill for £50,000 plus VAT, no he won't take a cheque.

Anyone with a scintilla of common sense and responsibility would go for option one. It would hurt for a while, but might just pay off in the long run. Unfortunately, there appears to be no one in the Cabinet with any common sense or responsibility whatsoever. It managed to run up debts of £50 billion. It employs twice as many people as it needs and spends far too much money it doesn't have. It is *our* money, never forget.

In short the government is living way beyond our means. But instead of doing the sensible thing – sacking hundreds of thousands of unnecessary civil servants, managers and outreach co-ordinators; closing superfluous ministries like the DTI, halting the spending of billions on everything from ludicrous health promotion schemes to buggering up every street in the country with red lego bricks and humps – the government called in the consultants. Not one firm of consultants. Not even two. In all seventeen thousand firms of consultants were hired. After twelve months, they managed to come up with savings of £10 million. That sounds a lot, but it's not much in the context of a debt of fifty thousand million pounds. Meanwhile the spending and hiring orgy goes on. The bill for all these consultants came to £565 million – more than fifty-six times what they saved. When challenged about all this absurd expenditure on consultants, John Major told the House of Commons that he thought it was very good value for money. And he used to work in a bank.

GETTING THE HUMP

As well as ordering an immediate freeze on public sector recruitment, the government should call a halt to the wasteful vandalisation of our streets and pavements. Despite pleading poverty and constantly whingeing about 'cuts' councils all over Britain seem to have a bottomless pit of money to waste on traffic humps and digging up perfectly good pavements to lay ghastly, ornamental paving schemes which no one asked for in the first place.

The country is disappearing under an avalanche of expensive little red bricks. Traffic-calming and fancy pavements are the physical manifestation of a society which has lost the plot completely. Never a financial year goes by without my local council announcing yet another package of cuts, hitting old folk, meals on wheels, libraries, nursery schools, all the usual targets. This usually happens just as the finishing touches are being put to yet another stretch of traffic humps or pavement 'improvements'. Now that most of the back-streets have been humped, councils are turning their attention to main roads. Not far from where I live, on a main road, within a quarter of a mile or so there are now half a dozen humps and a mini-roundabout at a junction with a little-used side road and a vast, pear-shaped island finished in ornamental red bricks. At a conservative estimate, based on conversations with friends in the building trade who have some experience of local government, the cost of this short stretch must have been somewhere around thirty grand by the time Town Hall overheads had been lumped in. Maybe more. That would be entirely consistent with a Department of Transport report which put the cost of each traffic hump in Britain at between £2000 and £5000, depending on the width of the road and the materials used. And naturally, when it comes to fashionable traffic 'calming' schemes, only the best materials are good enough for the highways department. It's not only the materials which are more expensive but labour charges are considerably higher. It takes eighteen little bricks to fill the space of a typical paving slab. Every road in the country will soon have more humps than a convention of Quasimodo impersonators. They are spreading like measles. Some councils have even taken to building humps out of little red bricks. Were I a little old lady about to be forcibly moved out of my sheltered accommodation and into a hostel, were I a school dinner lady about to be sacked, I would ask myself how it was that if the council were so hard up there was all this money for humps. And as both a motorist and a pedestrian I do ask myself why money can be found for humps but not for filling in holes in the road and repairing the pavement – and when roads are mended, any old rubbish, bits of wood, crisp packets and gravel will do.

So how is it that the supply of money for these schemes never dries up, even though virtually every other area of local government spending is curtailed? It works like this: humps come out of the 'calming' budget, which is government-backed and apparently a bottomless pit. Repairs come out of another budget altogether and have to take their chances alongside all the other 'services' councils supply. If councils don't spend all their humps money, they don't get so much next year. No one ever seems to look at the overall picture. Everything is taken in isolation, which is why you end up with the absurd situation of brand-new humps alongside gaping, months-old potholes. It happens everywhere. In the police, detectives find themselves sitting at home twiddling their thumbs because the overtime budget has run out. Yet there always seems to be plenty of cash available for helicopters, new Rovers and spy cameras. That's again because it comes out of different budgets. The same principle applies in hospitals, where untold millions are spent on the latest laser technology and space-age drugs, yet ward after ward is being shut down and tens of thousands of beds stand idle while people cry out for hip replacements and flu treatments. The simple fact of the matter is that, contrary to the widespread belief of professional complainers and full-time lobbyists always demanding more 'resources', we can't have everything. Choices have to be made. And that means matching conflicting demands to the size of the pot, determining priorities and taking difficult decisions. In a perfect world there would be sweeties for everyone. We do not live in a perfect world. That is why we must concentrate on providing money for what is fundamental – basic pensions, basic health care, basic education, basic law enforcement. Real policemen, not sleeping policemen, if you like. There should be an immediate halt called to the proliferation of traffic humps. For instance, it cost £19,000 to put two humps in Watling Street in the City of London to help enforce a 20mph speed limit. Yet there had only been one incident causing injury in Watling Street in the previous seven years. Traffic speed in central London averages seven miles per hour. So why was it necessary to spend £19,000 on two humps to stop cars going at three times that speed? Even the official figure of between £2000 and £5000 a hump is now being exceeded – yet even that seems pretty absurd, considering you only need a couple of barrow-loads of Tarmac to make one. But Tarmac humps are no longer considered good enough. The latest fashion is for bigger and better humps, made of ornamental brick, the size of Table Mountain. Unchecked, there will be humps at ten-yard intervals on every road from Land's End to John O'Groats, each more elaborate and expensive than the last. Car journeys will resemble a ride on a big dipper.

The other development you may have noticed wherever you go are those weird T-shaped formations on the pavement, made out of knobbly red slabs. They are taking over the entire country. These fancy paving slabs are the latest ingenious wheeze in the relentless drive to waste public money and create unnecessary jobs. They are supposed to be non-slip. In fact, they are so non-slip that you have to be careful you don't stub your toe and break your ankle. They are dangerous and uncomfortable to walk on, hideous to look at and ridiculously expensive. No one has ever been asked if they wanted them. They just appeared. My theory of how this happened is that someone in government responsible for road safety will have jetted off somewhere exotic on Concorde for an international conference, probably sponsored by the company which makes these paving slabs. In between gulping down Pina Coladas by the swimming pool and touching up the waitresses, someone else will have provided figures purporting to prove that 23 million people worldwide will die in the next five years from falling off pavements. Back in Britain our sun-tanned public servant will have convened another conference – in Harrogate or Brighton – of local council highways officers, at which he will produce these alarming figures together with a government directive to cut deaths through falling off pavements. At a free drinks reception, also sponsored by the paving slabs manufacturer, everyone decides that Something Must Be Done. To justify five days on the razz, knocking off their secretaries at a five-star hotel at the taxpayer's expense, the highways supremos agree to buy millions of these non-slip paving slabs and order the digging up of every street corner in Britain. There is a claim that all this is for the benefit of the blind, to let them know where pedestrian crossings are. But we already have bleeping noises at pelican crossings, so what is the point? And if they are for the benefit of the blind, why do they have to be red? The real point is that it provides jobs for otherwise unemployable public 'servants' and gives government another excuse to bleed us dry. Meanwhile, people continue to trip up on uneven and loose pavements and fall down holes in the road as councils claim they haven't got any money for repairs because of 'government cuts'. So we have to put up with the proliferation of bollards, cobbled islands and – inevitably – plenty of T-shape, non-slip, knobbly red paving slab formations, ugly new signposts and arrows on the road, whether we like it or not because no one in government – a Conservative government, remember – has the courage to say: stop.

PC TV

About every six months, the BBC issues a new report which says it is too middle-class, too elitist, too South of England. As a result of the latest report, the Beeb announced it was spending £85 million developing new programmes to make its output more relevant to young people, the regions and minorities. In future, a typical evening's viewing could look like this:

5.30 **VISUALLY-CHALLENGED DATE:** The popular matchmaking show for homosexuals and lesbians with learning difficulties.

6.00 **NEWS:** Read by Terry Christian and Rab C. Nesbitt.

6.30 **NOEL'S HOSTEL PARTY:** Noel Edmonds turns Crinkley Bottom into a refuge for battered wives.

7.00 **HOLIDAYS:** A group of young offenders and their social workers report on the best adventure holidays taxpayers' money can buy.

7.30 **THE NATIONAL LOTTERY:** Desmond Lynam with your essential guide to the state benefits system. Last week an unmarried mother of five won a new council house, £200 a week for life and a Ford Escort. Everyone's a winner!

8.00 **DRUG ADDICTS:** A brand-new show, based on the top-rated 'Telly Addicts'. Two teams of young people

inject themselves with an assortment of hard drugs
and then try to remember where they left the car they
stole earlier.

8.30   **FILM: Silence of the Lambs:** Remake of the Old
Brigitte Bardot classic, set in Yorkshire. A group of
animal rights demonstrators burn down Emmerdale
Farm.

10.00 **A QUESTION OF SPORT:** New series in which teams
of top footballers are asked: 'Do you plead guilty or
not guilty?' This week featuring Dennis Wise, Paul
Merson, Tony Adams and Paul Ince. Your host is
David Mellor.

11.30 **THE SOUTH BANK SHOW:** Melvyn Bragg shares a
drink with a group of dossers in Cardboard City. In
association with Special Brew.

12.30 **EPILOGUE:** Tonight, the Ayatollah of West Bromwich
calls for the death of Western civilisation.

I've just about given up on mainstream TV. These days I
take refuge in the satellite TV channel UK Gold, wallowing
in 1970s classics such as 'The Sweeney' and the early
episodes of 'Minder'. It is like harking back to a golden age
before political correctness. Just how far standards have
changed was demonstrated by the decision of ITV chiefs to
order cuts in the rerun first episode of 'Minder' last year
because it was considered offensive to women and blacks. I
couldn't help wondering what 'Minder' would be like if it
had to comply with 1995 PC rules.

The scene is the Winchester Club. Enter Arfur:
ARFUR: Evening, Dave. Large VAT, please.
DAVE: Sorry, Arfur.
ARFUR: What, no vodka?

DAVE: Oh, we've got vodka all right, Arfur. It's just that I can't serve you one.

ARFUR: If it's about the slate, Dave, I guarantee I will pay it off by the end of this week. I'm knocking out a G-reg Lada this very afternoon. Stand on me.

DAVE: It's not the slate, Arfur. I've been keeping a record of what you have been drinking and you have already exceeded your twenty-one units.

ARFUR: Units, Dave?

DAVE: Recommended weekly limit. You had yours yesterday lunchtime.

ARFUR: Who says so?

DAVE: Virginia Bottomley. I've had a visit from the health people. In future licensees will be fined up to £10,000 if they knowingly sell one of their punters more than the recommended limit. It's even less than that for birds. They're only allowed fourteen units.

ARFUR: Fourteen? 'Er Indoors gets through that during one episode of 'Home and Away.'

DAVE: And that's another thing, Arfur.

ARFUR: What now?

DAVE: 'Er Indoors. That is sexist language. The council inspectors came round the other day and said that premises permitting the use of language offensive to women will be closed down.

ARFUR: Oh, my good gawd. Is this what we fought two wars for? Give us a lardy.

DAVE: Sorry, Arfur. We're not allowed to cell cigars. This is a No Smoking establishment now.

ARFUR: David, this is supposed to be gentleman's club, a refuge from wives, where a chap can settle down with a Havana and fistful of finest falling-over fluid, ice and slice.

DAVE: Not any more, Arfur. According to the council we have to admit 50 per cent women members in future.

ARFUR: This is outrageous. I shall be writing to my MP. Packet of pork scratchings, please.

DAVE: 'Fraid not, Arfur. Pork scratchings is banned on account of being offensive to certain ethnic minorities.

Enter Cheerful Charlie Chisholm.

ARFUR: I suppose you've come to check for illegal Woodbines, sergeant.

CHISHOLM: Much as it would please me to nick you for possession of a packet of Whiffs, Daley, that is not the purpose of my visit. I have come to drown my sorrows.

ARFUR: Unless you can get Brahms on twenty-one units, you've come to the wrong place.

CHISHOLM: Actually, I did think for a moment I had come to the wrong place. Why does it say Mandela's over the door, Dave?

DAVE: We had a visit from the Fulham outreach co-ordinator of the Commission for Racial Equality. She said that the name The Winchester Club was Anglo-Saxist and racist and designed to discourage blacks from drinking here. She said unless I changed it to a council-approved name then I would be hauled up before the courts and sent to prison for five years.

ARFUR: Can you get shovel for having the wrong name these days?

CHISHOLM: It's about the only thing you can, Arfur. I collared Psycho Sid for the Chiswick security van job. He got off with three months.

ARFUR: In Parkhurst?

CHISHOLM: No, in Barbados. He was sentenced to three months' windsurfing.

DAVE: Weren't you up for promotion after that, Mr Chisholm?

CHISHOLM: Too right, Dave. Only they gave the inspector's job to a twenty-two-year-old black woman who failed the entrance exam to Hendon. Positive discrimination, they call it. Apparently they got the idea from 'The Bill'.

ARFUR: What can you expect from a Prime Minister who failed

the entrance exam for a No 14 bus? It is time to start on next week's units, Dave. This is an emergency.

DAVE: Just this once then, Arfur. But if anyone comes in you're to say it's Perrier.

Enter Ray.

RAY: Where do you want the condom machine in the Ladies, Dave?

ARFUR: Rubber johnnies in the Ladies? I don't know what the world is coming to.

DAVE: EC regulations, Arfur.

ARFUR: There might be an opening for Daley Into Europe, here. Ray, have we still got those boxes of Durex back in the lock-up?

RAY: They all passed their sell-by dates in 1986, Arfur.

ARFUR: A minor detail, Raymond. No one checks things like that when they're in the throes of legover.

CHISHOLM: Speaking of legover, whatever happened to Terry McCann?

ARFUR: We've not heard a word from him since he moved in with that bloke with the earring he met on the Anti-Nazi League march. Who'd have thought it? Terry, a brown-hatter.

DAVE: Less of the language, Arfur. Walls have ears.

ARFUR: So do horses, but they don't put jewelled studs through them. That's it, Dave, I've had enough. I'm retiring to the lock-up with a bottle of Smirnoff. See you on Friday.

DAVE: I don't think so, Arfur.

ARFUR: What do you mean, I always get in here on a Friday evening.

DAVE: Not no more, Arfur. From now on Friday night is Lesbian and Gay Night.

WANTED – FOR SARCASM

In the twenty-four years I've been in journalism, I've often written for the front page. But it took me twenty-two years to make front-page news myself. The day after Sydney was chosen as the venue for the next Olympic Games, I decided to devote the first hour of my LBC show to discussing the futility of the failed British bid. This time it was Manchester's turn to make up the numbers, just as it had been Birmingham's four years earlier. Millions of pounds of taxpayers' money were frittered away on a ludicrous sales pitch which never stood a cat in hell's chance. My opening monologue went like this:

> Once again the plucky little Brits fought a brave campaign – and once again we got stuffed. The presence of John Major was simply the custard on the crumble. Hopeless but honest – a motto for a nation. Whatever possessed anyone to think that the International Olympic Committee would rather tuck into a doner kebab and chips in Salford at the side of the ship canal when they could be dining on red snapper overlooking Sydney Harbour? Manchester simply doesn't compare. Admittedly it does have a marginally better human rights record than Peking and, to be fair, I understand there is a half-decent Berni Inn at the back of the central bus depot. But people in Altrincham and Bolton

*don't want to go to Manchester if they can possibly avoid it.
So what made anyone else think that the rest of the world
would be queuing up to go there?*

*Manchester is a dull, provincial city with one decent
football team, and 'Coronation Street' and, er, that's about
it. It was a complete waste of time and money. Sixty million
quid and what have the people of Manchester got to show for
it? A massive debt and a half-finished bike track, that's what.
It is time we gave up these ridiculous and ill-fated regional
bids. London is the only British city capable of winning and
hosting the Olympics. It is a world-class city, not a scruffy,
rundown leftover from the industrial revolution. About the
only thing you can say for Manchester is that it isn't
Liverpool . . .*

There was more in a similar vein. While I was speaking, in
the background we played Monty Python's 'Always Look
on The Bright Side of Life' – which the disappointed hordes
gathered in the centre of Manchester the night before had
been singing as the ubiquitous Northern rain fell on their
parade. This was all in a fairly light-hearted vein. It was
Friday, after all. But there was a serious point underlying it.
I was only trying to be honest. Mind you, I should have
known better. Telling the truth has got me in enough
trouble over the years. This was no exception.

Now, the only reason I can remember quite so accurately
what I actually said is that the following morning my
remarks were splashed all over the front page of the
Northern editions of the *Daily Mirror*. And for good
measure, *Mirror* readers who had missed my monologue –
in other words, every single reader of the *Daily Mirror*
outside LBC's London and Home Counties transmission
area –could hear it for themselves by dialling 0891 111 299
and listening to a tape recording made by some enterprising

Mirror executive (calls charged at 36p off-peak, 48p at all other times). I may have been speaking in my capacity as a London radio talk-show host and addressing my stream of consciousness to an exclusively Southern audience. But I had reckoned without the circulation war between the *Sun* and the *Mirror*.

NORTH RAGES AGAINST SUN HACK'S BLAST, screamed the headline. '*Sun* newspaper columnist Richard Littlejohn savagely kicked the city of Manchester when it was down yesterday – then put the boot in to Liverpool, too,' the *Mirror* reported, attempting to link my remarks to the *Sun*'s coverage of the behaviour of Liverpool fans at the Hillsborough disaster, which led to a boycott of the paper on Merseyside. (I wasn't at the *Sun* at the time of Hillsborough. I was still with the *Evening Standard*. Mind you, I did get reported to the Press Council over my *Standard* column about Hillsborough. Found Not Guilty, surprisingly, since you ask. This was before it became a crime against political correctness to utter a single syllable of criticism of Liverpool or Liverpudlians.)

The *Mirror* rounded up the usual suspects to put the boot into me and The Currant Bun. A parade of professional Northerners had their three-penn'orth. Gerry Marsden, the former lead singer of Gerry and The Pacemakers and a man without whom no disaster would be complete, raged: 'It's absolute stupidity.' 'Coronation Street' actor Ken Morley, who plays Reg Holdsworth, said: 'I look forward to seeing Littlejohn up here. Tell him we still have hanging.' Comedian Stan Boardman added: 'I can't believe anyone would run down the North like this.' All good knockabout stuff, and if it helped get Gerry, Stan and Ken a few more gigs opening supermarkets, so much the better. No hard feelings. All's fair in love and circulation wars.

A couple of days later at the Labour Party conference in

Brighton, I was ambushed in the bar by a television crew from Granada TV. They had been sent all the way there to front me up. An earnest and indignant young man pushed a microphone in my face and demanded that I explain myself to his viewers. I owed the people of Manchester an apology, he insisted. On the contrary, I replied, people like him and Manchester City Council owed an apology to the people of Manchester for conning them into believing that they ever stood a chance of hosting the Olympics. I had nothing against Manchester, in fact I rather liked both the city and the people who live there, I continued, but the truth of the matter was that it simply isn't a world–class city to compare with the likes of Barcelona, Sydney and Los Angeles. End of story. Nothing personal. But if only the government would put more 'resources' into the region, he countered, chanting the usual local television reporter's Question Four. Where were these 'resources' to come from? He looked puzzled. Er, the government. I explained patiently that sixty million quid had already been tipped into a black hole and all the city had to show for it was a half-finished bike track and some sun-tanned local councillors. He went away to edit his scoop. With any luck it would bring him to the attention of ITN and he could get a nice job in London and not have to waste his time covering complete bollocks. If he had been a little more eagle-eyed he might have noticed David Seymour, assistant editor of the *Daily Mirror*, slipping away from the bar with his collar up. We'd been having a pint and a laugh about me adorning the front page of his august organ when the arc lights had been switched on.

The following week I was having a livener in the bar of the Imperial Hotel in Blackpool at the Tory conference when John Gummer, the Environment Secretary and member for Vatican East, joined me. 'I've just been to

Liverpool,' he said. 'There's a picture of you on every bus stop in the north-west.' Oh yeah, I suppose you want a drink while you're here. 'It's true,' he assured me. It turned out the *Mirror* had commissioned a poster campaign with a great big, ugly mug shot of me next to a huge *Sun* logo and the words: 'The only thing you can say for Manchester is that it isn't Liverpool' and 'What the *Sun* really thinks of the North' – totally ignoring the fact that none of this had been said in the *Sun* or by the *Sun*. Talk about things getting out of hand. I'm sure it seemed a good idea at the time. The amazing thing about all this is not so much the way the *Mirror* acted. I was fair game and it was all a bit of a chuckle. No harm done. What amazes me is the way in which some northern cities reacted with such umbrage at any slight. Phone-ins, letters to MPs, questions in the House. Who gives a monkey's? In the same edition of the *Mirror*, councillors were demanding an apology from Paddy Pantsdown after he had described Moss Side as 'poor, neglected and overwhelmed by crime'. Sounds about right to me. If some local disc jockey in Manchester had criticised some aspect of London, no one would have taken the slightest bit of notice. This is the way small towns react, not world-class cities. I rest my case.

Later in the week of the Labour conference, I was sharing a couple of large ones with a North-West Labour MP of my acquaintance. 'You were absolutely right,' he said, 'but don't you bloody quote me.' So what had Manchester got for sixty million quid, over and above the aforementioned bike track? 'Bugger all,' he replied. 'But all my mates on Manchester council have had a few good holidays flying round the world at the taxpayers' expense.' Now that *is* a front-page story.

Footnote: When I started my Sky TV show in September 1994, one of the first people I ran into in the bar at the Millbank studios in Westminister was the Granada reporter who had challenged me on my views of Manchester. He is now working for the BBC in London. You couldn't make it up, you really couldn't.

THE LAST POST

Britain has the most efficient Post Office in the world. It is far from perfect, but it makes a profit as well as performing an admirable public service. Plans to privatise it were put on hold after a concerted protest campaign. But if I know President Heseltine, like Arnie, he'll be back. The only reason the Tories want to flog it off is to raise money to offset the billions lost through their own financial incompetence and bring in enough to cut taxes – which they increased – in the belief we are stupid enough to swallow an election bribe and gratefully re-elect them.

If the eventual privatisation of the Post Office followed the same pattern as the sell-off of the other former nationalised industries it will go something like this:

1 Hire Sir Tim Bell on a £1 million retainer.
2 Hire a firm of stockbrokers which makes substantial donations to the Tory Party to prepare sale. Fees: £60 million.
3 Hire advertising agency which makes substantial donations to the Tory party to co-ordinate campaign. Fees: £3 million.
4 Spend £500 million on media advertising campaign, making sure adverts are placed with companies which make substantial donations to the Tory Party.
5 Sell shares at £1 a time to mug punters.

6 Mug punters make a quick profit by selling their shares at £1.50 to big companies which make substantial donations to the Tory Party.

7 Chairman of Post Office trebles salary.

8 Directors of Post Office treble their salaries.

9 Chairman and directors of Post Office given share options worth £25 million.

10 Post Office calls in firm of image consultants which makes substantial donations to the Tory Party. Fees: £5 million.

11 Post Office changes name to PO.

12 All Post Offices, headquarters, vans etc. redesigned, repainted and refurbished by firms which make substantial donations to the Tory Party. Cost £500 million.

13 Red pillar boxes ripped out and replaced by turquoise bins.

14 PO announces that 50,000 postmen are to be made redundant to save money.

15 Cost of stamp goes up to 50p. It replaces the old First Class and Second Class.

16 PO announces that since the two services have now been merged, next-day delivery is being scrapped.

17 PO announces a new Executive Class stamp costing £5, guaranteeing next-day delivery, but only in cities. Deliveries in rural areas cease.

18 OAPs to be charged £10 admission to collect pensions.

19 Two thousand PO counters closed. PO blames lack of demand. Another 10,000 jobs go.

20 PO announces record profits of £1500 million.

21 Chairman and directors quadruple their salaries.

22 Michael Heseltine joins the board of the PO.

23 PO sold to the Germans.

SIRUS THE VIRUS

You will all have heard of Lenny the Lion, Biffo the Bear, Dennis the Menace, Muffin the Mule, Larry the Lamb and Kermit the Frog. But I bet you've never heard of Sirus the Virus – or Sirus the HIV Virus to give him his full name. I promise I am not making this up. Sirus was invented by the Rubber Johnny Police in Somerset to star in 10,000 magazines warning junior schoolchildren about the dangers of AIDS. To be honest, I wasn't aware that junior schoolchildren were considered a high-risk group. But better safe than sorry. You never know when the average Somerset schoolboy might be tempted to nip behind the bike sheds to inject himself with heroin from a dirty syringe or play doctors and nurses without a condom.

Sirus came to my attention when he was withdrawn, following a complaint from a real-life Mr Sirus, who thought his family would be tainted by association with the virulent cartoon creature. It gets better, doesn't it. I was surprised that Somerset health officials didn't come up with an equally charming replacement. How about: Lester the Child Molester?

There are a couple of aspects of this episode which give grounds for concern. If the alarming reports from the Department of Education are to be believed, very few children can even spell AIDS. Apparently, one in four seven-year-olds cannot recognise three letters of the alphabet and one in three is incapable of counting up to 100. You might just have thought the authorities in Somerset, and everywhere else for that matter, would be better employed ensuring that children can read, write and add up before trying to fill their heads with sexually transmitted diseases. (All this nonsense coming at a time when education budgets were under pressure and schools were talking about closing classrooms and sacking qualified and experienced teachers). But no. Proper education has been replaced by political and sexual brainwashing. We can't, of course, let our children grow up in blissful ignorance. Nor can we shield them indefinitely from the seamier side of life. There are some sick warped people about. The trouble is half of them seem to be working either for the local council or some pressure group or other. There was another story about a child welfare activist attacking Marks & Spencer for selling satin knickers to little girls on the grounds that it will encourage perverts. Would that have occurred to you? Me neither. It takes a special kind of mind to make that sordid link. But back to AIDS.

It came as no great surprise to me to learn that there are now more people making a living out of AIDS than there are dying from it. AIDS has replaced race relations and wheel clamping as the great growth industry of our age. In Manchester, where just eighteen people were reported to have the disease, £2.73 million is being spent on AIDS in a single year. That is considerably more than the amount allocated in the entire North West to breast cancer, which affects one in twelve women. Where there's death, there's a nice little drink in it for someone. One man's illness is another man's meal ticket. No wonder AIDS victims are modern heroes, like the revolting film director Derek Jarman, who died of the disease which he probably contracted while 'cruising' Hampstead Heath. In order better to serve the 'gay community', and presumably to provide a fitting memorial for Jarman, the Camden and Islington Health Authority, in conjunction with the Barnet Health Authority and the Camden HIV Unit, set up a stall on Hampstead Heath to distribute condoms to homosexuals who gather there for casual sex. The *Independent* once ran a feature on the open-air orgy taking place nightly in the shadow of Kenwood and Jack Straw's Castle, providing a layman's guide to such exotic locations as 'Gobblers' Gulch' and 'The Yum-Yum Tree'. I have no wish for anyone to die as a result of their sexuality, but I can see nothing heroic about being buggered by a complete stranger in a public place. And I refuse to accept that it is the job of the NHS to encourage this disgusting behaviour. Or the job of local authorities, either. But while Somerset was spending a fortune inventing Sirus the Virus and warning schoolchildren of the dangers of catching AIDS, Nottingham council was spending £30,000 on an arts exhibition celebrating the lifestyle most likely to lead you to contract the disease. Nottingham's 'Cottaging Through The Ages' exhibition, featuring homosexuals chatting each other up in public conveniences, was staged in a disused toilet, which the council said it hadn't got enough money to keep open. You really couldn't make this stuff up, could you?

Virginia Bottomley is much maligned, but she was absolutely right to cut the amount of money spent on AIDS propaganda. Not that the fight against AIDS should be neglected, but it is a question of proportion and priorities. Predictions of a heterosexual AIDS epidemic have proved to be groundless scaremongering. At the last count, there were only sixty-three recorded cases outside high-risk groups. It was always folly to spend £900 million scaring young heterosexual men and women half to death, even if it did wonders for condom sales. That was like targeting lung cancer adverts at non-smokers or anti-booze ads to tee-totallers. The money which has been, and continues to be, wasted on AIDS propaganda is staggering. For instance, something calling itself the South East London Health Promotions Service decided to organise a Condom Skills seminar. Honestly. I promise you I'm not making this up, ridiculous as it sounds. It was in the *Observer*, so it must be true. The course was designed for health service staff, youth workers and other professionals employed in 'the encouraging of others to use condoms', and was organised to give lessons in the 'correct protocol, selection and use of condoms'. Their words. Delegates will discuss the merits of the assorted sheaths currently available, including the ribbed and flavoured varieties. Presumably, there will be some kind of tasting during the lunch break. I couldn't help wondering how far the instruction went. 'Just once more, Nurse Goodbody, we haven't tried the green ones with the knobbly bits yet. I know it's a nuisance but lie back and think of the NHS.' It's a dirty and dangerous job but someone's got to do it. Miss Frankie Lynch, Commissioner of the South East London Rubber Johnny Police, justified this ludicrous event thus: 'It is quite surprising what can go wrong. Air bubbles get in. Men forget to unroll them. Some even try to put them on when they are . . . well, when they are still limp. When a condom fails, women conceive, or worse still, AIDS is transmitted,' she told the *Observer*. Well, knock me down with a Featherlite. Thank heavens we've got people like Frankie Lynch watching out for us. We were not told how much this seminar cost but you can bet on a few grand.

Miss Lynch believes in being generous with our National Insurance contributions. 'If a woman goes to her GP's surgery and asks for condoms, there is no point in giving her a couple. She may be going away for a month's holiday. She may need ten packets.' This came as news to me, and perhaps it does to you too. Do doctors really hand out free packets-of-three to everyone heading off on a Club 18–30 knees-up? More to the point, if a woman wants to jet to the sun and sleep with a different dago waiter every night why should we be expected to pay for it? It's not as if condoms are difficult to get hold of these days. The embarrassing 'something for the weekend, sir?' days are over. Every pub has at least one machine in the gents' selling three for a quid. I'm told they also have them in the ladies'. Apparently they flog them in schools, too. For all I know, you get them free in Lucky Bags. And you're spoiled for choice – everything from Malibu flavour to luminous designer sheaths which glow in the dark and fearsome things which look like medieval instruments of torture. Call me old-fashioned, but they're not my idea of a night out.

I once gave an after-dinner speech to franchisees of the London Rubber Company and sat next to a woman who said she had been involved in testing some of the flavoured variety. She couldn't explain why, however, you can get chocolate flavour but not cheese'n'onion. No call for it, I suppose. If people like Miss Frankie Lynch had their way, every pub toilet would have a resident condom advice outreach worker. We would all be forced to attend counselling sessions and Condom Skills conferences before obtaining an official leg-over licence. Anyone discovered not using a condom would face a fine of up to £10,000 and six months in prison.

Having identified the problem of men who forget to unroll them or try to put them on when they are still limp, it may have also crossed Miss Lynch's mind that this is because sex regularly occurs when both parties have had a few. I wouldn't put it past the South East London Health Promotions Service to start employing teams of index-linked condom inspectors to mount late-night raids in our bedrooms and administer compulsory breath tests and supervise the rolling-on of condoms before any act of sexual intercourse can take place. This may all sound daft, but in light of the current debate about public spending cuts, prescription charges and forcing patients to pay for hospital beds, it is worth asking what the hell is going on in the health service.

The NHS and the concept of free health care for all is a wonderful idea, but somewhere along the line the basic plot has been lost. Unless I am mistaken, rubber johnnies all round were not in the original script. Neither, I am absolutely positive, if you'll pardon the expression, was Sirus the Virus.

THE RACIST CAPTAIN SCARLET

The Commission for Racial Equality is a regular contributor to the You Couldn't Make It Up files. One of its most absurd pronouncements was the declaration that the puppet character Captain Scarlet was 'racist'. Where do they find these people? The Commission supported a complaint from Bristol councillor Mohammed Khali Ahmed that the show was having a 'very negative effect on race relations in this country' because one of the baddies is called Captain Black.

The day the story broke, I invited Captain Scarlet's creator, Gerry Anderson – the man behind everything from 'Stingray' to 'Thunderbirds' – on to my LBC radio programme to defend himself. Mr Anderson was livid. He questioned whether Mohammed Khali Ahmed or anyone at the CRE has ever seen the show. Because, he pointed out, if they had they would have known that Captain Black is white. Furthermore, two of the good guys in the programme are black. And in the sixties, when the programme was made, this was enough to get it banned from some segregationist Southern states in the USA. Mr Anderson came under pressure to change the pigmentation, but stuck to his principles even though it cost him a great deal of money. Advertisers fought shy of the show in some States because it was thought to portray inflammatory images.

But today's redneck racists are bigots like Mohammed Khali Ahmed and the members of the CRE, who seek out racism where it doesn't exist and see poison in innocent children's puppet shows. We were flooded with calls from indignant listeners, wanting to know what the thought police would try to ban next. Someone suggested 'Blackadder' and Cilla Black. I asked, tongue-in-cheek, where that left the Black Dyke Mills Band? Racist, heterosexist – or what? I should have known better. The following week it was reported that officials at Carnegie Hall, in New York – where the Black Dyke Mills Band was due to perform – had written to the band to ask if they would mind changing their name to the British Mills Band, so as not to offend lesbians of the African-American persuasion.

Footnote: On the day I was due to deliver this book to my publishers, it was reported that there were demands for tens of thousands of Bugs Bunny videos to be withdrawn from sale in the USA on the grounds that they were offensive to Japanese Americans. Don't even ask. Slant eyes and buck teeth, I suppose.

You really couldn't make it up.

THE BOTTLE ANSWERS BACK

Where would the newspapers be without My Battle With The Bottle? Barely a week passes without yet another celebrity emerging from a drying-out clinic to talk about his (or, equally likely, her) victory over the demon drink. But there are two sides to every story. After reading about Michael Barrymore's spell in a rehabilitation clinic, I decided it was time for The Bottle to answer back and give his side of the story . . .

I tracked The Bottle down to the exclusive Dom Perignon bottle bank in Malibu, where he checked in to escape the publicity surrounding his relationship with Michael Barrymore. Looking tanned and fit, and sporting a new label and screw top, The Bottle spoke frankly for the first time about his stormy life with the stars:

'It all began in 1966, in Swinging London. It was the year of the World Cup in England and I used to hang out with a lot of footballers. That was when I first met Jimmy Greaves. He was a smashing bloke. He would take me to matches with him and smuggle me into the dressing room for a quick swig in the showers before the kick-off. Jimmy was on top of his game then, scoring goals like there was no tomorrow. He used to say I gave him strength. But then it all went wrong after he was dropped from the World Cup final team. He took it out on me, hitting me every minute of the day. I couldn't take any more. After that I moved in with George Best for a while. He couldn't keep his hands off me. I was the envy of every bottle in Britain. But we eventually split up when he went to prison. Last I heard of him he had moved in with a pint of Guinness in Hammersmith.

'Then there was Jimi Hendrix. He would stick his fingers in my neck and slide me along the strings of his guitar, but he chucked me for drugs and the rest is history. The seventies were a difficult time for bottles. After Brian Jones was found floating face down in his swimming pool we went out of fashion. Most of the pop stars were only interested in uppers and downers and heroin. I remember Keith Moon, of The Who, saying he wanted some coke. But when I suggested a bottle of Pepsi, he went mental and threw me out of the window, along with the TV set, a table lamp and the bed. Fortunately, I landed in a bush and survived. After that, I'd had it with pop stars.

'I began mixing with actors and comedians. That was the first time I went with a woman. Yootha Joyce, her name was. It was the same old story. At first it was brilliant. She used to have me in her dressing room before the show and again when the recording was finished. Sometimes she even nipped out for a quickie during the commercial break. But when the ratings started to fall, she blamed me. The only other woman I've ever had a relationship with was Paula Hamilton. She picked me up at a film première. I'd never heard of her before, though apparently she was once in a commercial for Volkswagen. I wouldn't know. Drink and driving don't mix in my book. Paula was a real raver. I used to call her Martini – any time, any place, anywhere. She was insatiable. She once had me in the back of a minicab. When I couldn't give her any more, she went berserk and smashed up the cab. Then she had the cheek to blame me. I've got used to carrying the can over the years. A couple of months ago I saw a picture of her with an elephant. Elephant's trunk again, I thought to myself.

'I met Jim Davidson in a club in south London. We've had a very close relationship over the years, but women keep coming between us. We'd be out on the town, he'd meet some bird, marry her and that would be the last I'd see of him for a few weeks. He always comes back to me though. With Michael Barrymore it was love at first sight. In the beginning he was very gentle with me, but then as his career took off he would want me more and more often. It became so that he couldn't bear to be apart from me. Even when I was empty, he wasn't satisfied. He would grab me by the neck, hold me upside down and shake me. I couldn't keep up with him. Sometimes I would sneak out of the house to get five minutes' peace. I even tried hiding in the boot of his car, but he always found me in the end. One night we sat down and agreed on a trial separation. Michael checked into the Ashley Centre, in Maryland, and I came here. I like it here in Malibu. I came once before when Jim married Alison Holloway. When that didn't work out, after about a week, he sent for me and I moved back in with him. I expect he'll be back in touch any day now. Here, isn't that Don Johnson over there?'

YOU'RE NICKED

Someone calculated that it will take an extra 406 days in police time every year to read out the new sixty-word caution to suspects. Still, it could have been worse. I have it on good authority that this was the original draft:

> Excuse me, sir/madam. I really am most sorry to disturb you but we would be extremely grateful if you could see your way to helping us with our enquiries – at your convenience of course.
>
> You have the right to a chauffeur-driven limousine to the station.
>
> You have the right to a social worker.
>
> You have the right to the most expensive legal advice money can buy, all at the taxpayer's expense. Would you like me to call George Carman before we begin?
>
> I must caution you that anything I say will be written down and may be used against me when you accuse me of fitting you up. You have the right to compensation and, if convicted, the right to a holiday of your choice anywhere in the world. I hear Belize is nice at this time of year, but if you don't fancy flying – Club Class, naturally – Center Parcs is a jolly nice alternative.

Is there anything else I can do for you, sir/ madam? A nice cup of tea perhaps? Or something a little stronger? I know how difficult this all is for you. You could always have a lie down before we continue. My pleasure. No, no, please don't say anything which could get you into trouble.

Call me an old-fashioned sentimentalist, but I can't see what's wrong with: 'You're nicked.'

COMING TO GRIEF

Within hours of the horrific 1993 minibus crash on the M40 which killed a number of children from Hagley Roman Catholic School on their way back from a concert in London, their classrooms were crawling with disaster counsellors. They were there even before the school gates opened, though the crash had only happened in the early hours of the morning. Hereford and Worcester Council despatched a team of ten. Others came crawling out of the woodwork from all over the Midlands. 'We are going through the classes one by one. We are not just here for today, or this week, or this month, or this year,' their leader promised. In other words, these unfortunate children were never going to be allowed to forget their sorrow.

Leaflets were distributed to pupils, parents, teachers, friends and relatives telling them how they were expected to grieve. It makes you wonder how we coped before. In the case of the Hagley minibus tragedy, I'd have thought a tight-knit Roman Catholic community would be better equipped than most to cope with such a trauma – especially with the support of families and the church. Why the hell should they need para-counselling squads of *Guardian* readers to give them a shoulder to cry on?

People have been coping with grief for centuries without recourse to psycho-babble. The British are renowned for their stoicism, their stiff upper lip. It is one of the characteristics which distinguishes us from the weeping and wailing and gnashing of teeth of the Southern Europeans and the whirling dervishes. Where would we have been during the Blitz if, every time a bomb had landed on the East End, it had been attended not by ARPs and fire-wardens but by hundreds of men in duffle coats urging all and sundry to let it all out? How would we ever have liberated Port Stanley if the troops involved in yomping across the Falkland Islands had to sit down with a counsellor for a fortnight every time one of their comrades was shot?

Death and its aftermath are part of the human condition. We grieve, we recover, we remember, we forget. That's the deal. We have managed quite nicely up to now, thank you very much. Children, in particular, are adept at handling tragedy. Their youth and lack of self-pity helps them quickly overcome adversity and the loss of a close friend. The sooner they forget and resume normal life, the better. What the pupils of Hagley Roman Catholic School needed was to hug each other, to cry, to grieve in private with their friends and families. But ghoulish counsellors have a vested interest in making sure the bereaved are not allowed to forget. They want to keep reminding them of their trauma. Perhaps they take pleasure in immersing themselves in the despair and distress of others.

Of course, if people were allowed to grieve in private, there would be no need for grief counsellors on twenty-five grand a year plus. What we are seeing yet again is an exercise in job creation for otherwise unemployable members of the polytechnocracy, equipped with worthless degrees and diplomas in sociology and psychology. It goes something like this. Someone sits down one day and identifies a need. Conferences are held at the taxpayers' expense, called things like Combating The Grief

Syndrome. Seminars are held in four-star hotels and college campuses, with the usual ration of cheap red wine, vol-au-vents and shagging. They are conducted by insane American academics, still recovering from the acid they took at Woodstock. They spend three hours talking complete bollocks to an impressionable audience drawn from the outreach departments of local authorities and the National Health Service. Bogus figures are produced, based on a study in Des Moines, Iowa, to prove that grief is a major threat to public health and costs every man, woman and child in the country £10,000 a year in lost days and work and medicines. The only way to counteract this growing problem, which will have reached epidemic proportions in five years' time, is to establish a nationwide network of professional counsellors on call twenty-four hours a day. Within weeks, the office space has been allocated, the job ads are placed in the *Guardian* and the company cars have been ordered. The next time there is a car crash in Wisbech, a man with a beard and no qualifications whatsoever from something called the Professional Institute of Grief Counselling appears on 'About Anglia' insisting that unless more 'resources' are allocated to counselling immediately, millions will die/the earth will catch fire/there will be a plague of boils/perm any one you like. Next thing you know, Wisbech council has a department of two dozen counsellors making a bloody nuisance of themselves, racing the fire brigade to rescue cats up trees and console the owners.

Counselling is just another manifestation of the belief that the State knows best, and that any problem has an emotional or psychological root cause and cure. It also helps convince people that they need take no responsibility for their own welfare and that someone, or something, else is always to blame. Of course, all this needs expensive professional help.

Counselling has now infiltrated the heart of the NHS. Between 1987 and 1994, the number of registered counsellors practising in Britain increased from 3451 to 10,700 – with new members joining the British Association for Counselling at the rate of 300 a month. There are more counsellors in this country than there are stipendiary priests. In addition, according to a report from the Social Affairs Unit, there are a further 40,000 people dispensing full-time 'advice, guidance and counselling'. And you and I are picking up the bill. The Government is to blame. In 1990 it allowed GPs, through local authorities, to claim up to 70 per cent of the costs of hiring counsellors to work in their practices. Ministers believed that if all the malingerers and lead-swingers who clutter up doctors' surgeries could be palmed off with a counselling session for ten minutes, then cost savings could be made. Of course, it doesn't ever work like that. Once counsellors had got their foot in the door, they multiplied like rabbits – daily identifying new illnesses and 'needs' to be served. An essentially passive, responsive role inevitably became the aggressive 'pro-active' one – leading to the obscene haste and scale of the response to the Hagley minibus case. The decision to pay for counselling out of the already stretched NHS set a dangerous precedent. Instead of medicine and diagnosis, patients are now offered consolation, placebo and untested theory. It amounts to giving the lonely and disturbed a friend. Is that really what the NHS is supposed to be about? Isn't that what youth clubs and Dateline are for? While it poses as a profession, you don't need any special qualifications to set up in the counselling business. And there is evidence from some quarters to suggest that such therapy can actually be positively harmful. What good can it do to keep forcing a child to relive constantly the most horrific incident of his life? Everyone, it seems, now needs counselling. TV news reports regularly begin with the words: 'Teams of counsellors are standing by . . .' to deal with policemen and firemen attending motorway pile-ups, house fires, plane crashes etc. I'm sorry, but if police and fire officers need to cry on the shoulder of a *Guardian* reader in a duffle coat every time they have to clear up something they are paid for, then they shouldn't be in the job in the first place. If they're a bit upset they can have a chat with their sergeant or the station chaplain. There is another, sinister aspect to all this. Once psychological harm has been established a case for compensation often follows. So the taxpayer ends up paying to identify a need which doesn't exist, paying for someone to treat it and then paying compensation to the 'victim'.

Counselling is a classic displacement activity. In the same way doctors are using counsellors to get rid of problem patients, so chief constables are using them as a substitute for catching criminals. A friend of mine had his mobile phone stolen by thieves who smashed a window of his car, parked in an affluent suburb of North London where beat bobbies patrol about as regularly as knife-grinders and French onion sellers. He reported the crime, as you do, but was told there was little hope of the thief being apprehended or the phone recovered. Not that he gave a monkey's. The car and the phone belonged to his company. Within twelve hours he had had the window repaired and a new phone delivered to his office. This was not an incident over which he lost any sleep. The following day he received a letter from the Old Bill. It was from the victim support unit. It asked if he would like counselling.

Everyone's getting in on the act. Everyone in the public sector, that is. You don't get much of this nonsense in the private sector. Naturally, when it comes to wasting tax-payers' money, the BBC is in the van. The Beeb decided to offer stress counselling to staff involved in the D–Day coverage. Honestly. Phil Gilbert, the D–Day co-ordinator (why are they always co-ordinators?), says: 'Programme-making can be harrowing.' As one soldier remarked: 'They should try it with bullets.' Can you imagine what it would be like if the BBC had been running D–Day for real?

We're going in now, sir.

Not yet, Carruthers. The Sappers haven't finished the wheelchair access on Omaha beach.

Wheelchair access, sir?

Yes, Carruthers. For the differently abled members of the Royal Marines.

Who's in the advanced guard, sir?

We're sending a team of outreach co-ordinators to try to negotiate with the Germans. We've decided to try counselling before we send in the Paras.

The Parachute Regiment, sir?

No, the Paraplegic Support Unit. They're coming over from Omaha beach once they've adapted the latrines. They're all we've got.

What happened to the heavy artillery, sir?

On strike, I'm afraid. They're demanding parity with the Lesbian Resources Unit.

And the infantry?

They're on a racism awareness course at Sandhurst.

How are we going to slow a German counter-attack without the big guns?

Traffic-calming, Carruthers. We're building humps on the other side of those sand dunes. Roger. Before we do, Carruthers, have I ever told you how damned attractive I find you? If we get out of this alive, will you marry me?

Oh, yes, sir. Just think of all the things we can buy with our £75 honeymoon voucher.

OK, luvvies, that's a wrap. Everyone report to the stress counsellor before scene two.

Footnote: At the time I imagined the idea of a battalion of paraplegics in the army, I was joking. By February 1995, a concerted campaign was underway to make the armed forces accept disabled recruits. Michael Portillo, the then employment secretary, was coming under fire from militant disabled groups for trying to exempt the services from the full impact of the Disability Bill. He wanted occupations such as the police, the army, navy and RAF, the fire service and the prison service to be excluded on the grounds that these are jobs only suitable for people with a full complement of physical and mental faculties. This was being described as blatant discrimination and a court challenge was threatened. If the campaigners succeed, it will mean the services would have to employ blind pilots, one-legged firemen and wheelchair-bound paratroopers. And if you think I'm being ridiculous, remember: you couldn't make it up.

THE BEAUTIFUL GAME

Professional football is a beautiful game played by thugs and cheats and run by spivs and weak incompetents. Despite the improvement in stadia since the Hillsborough disaster and the formation of the Premier League, bringing some of the world's finest players to England, soccer hit its nadir in the 1994–95 season. English fans rioted in Dublin, Chelsea fans rioted in Bruges. The funniest aspect of the Bruges riot was that days earlier the actor Stephen Fry had run away to this beautiful medieval Belgian city to escape the pressures of the theatrical life. Fry disappeared from the Albery Theatre complaining about hostile reviews. The peace and calm of Bruges must have seemed the perfect haven from the backbiting of London's Luvvie Land. I couldn't help wondering how he must have felt when the windows of his hotel were stoved in by a team of skinheads from the council flats off the King's Road. Perhaps they were chanting: 'Stevie Fry's blue and white army!' Poor Stephen, darling. Oh, the noise, the people! With the Belgian police rounding up everything with an English accent, I half expected Fry to have been caught up in the riot. I sat by my TV waiting to see pictures of him being escorted on to a ferry at Ostend, handcuffed to a riot cop, surrounded by earringed plankton in football shirts, protesting loudly: 'You've made a terrible mistake, sweetie. I'm an act–OR.'

But there weren't many moments of light relief during the season. Violence returned to the pitch as well as the terraces. There were boardroom upheavals, investigations by the Inland Revenue and the 'bung' scandal which cost Arsenal manager George Graham his job after eight-and-a-half successful years at Highbury, following revelations that he had accepted unsolicited gifts totalling £425,000 from transfer dealings. At the time of writing, the 'bung' investigations threatened to bring with them a few more high-profile casualties.

Manchester United unveiled its fifth kit in two years – blue and white shirts and shorts. This from a team calling itself 'The Red Devils'. Yet the mug punters queued up to buy it. A Geordie friend of mine, living in the south, took his five-year-old son to his first Newcastle United match at Chelsea. The boy was kitted out from head to foot in the traditional black and white stripes of the Magpies. The team took the pitch wearing yellow and green. When did you last see a yellow and green magpie? On my Sky TV show, I interviewed an unemployed Geordie fan who had paid £120 out of his dole money to have a picture of the Newcastle striker Andy Cole tattooed on his thigh – three days before Cole was transferred to Manchester United for £7 million. Mind you, I don't know what I was laughing at. I've got a Labrador called Ossie. I spent six months after Ossie Ardiles was sacked by Spurs trying to get the dog to answer to the name Jurgen.

United signed Cole to partner the Frenchman Eric Cantona. A couple of games later, Cantona flew into the crowd at Selhurst Park and kung fu kicked a fan – resulting, after much prevarication, in a heavy fine and an eight-month ban by the Football Association, and, at time of writing, a pending appearance in court on assault charges. Cantona wasn't the only United player involved in the

Selhurst Park violence, as I was reminded watching the
disturbances at the game between England and Ireland at
Landsdowne Road, in Dublin, a few weeks earlier. One
image stood out. It was not the blind hatred etched into
every crag of the shaven-headed plankton spitting venom,
throwing punches and hurling missiles. Nor was it the
blood pouring down the head of a ginger-haired spectator
clubbed by police, nor the fear and bewilderment of the
young Irish fan in his green and white scarf, featured in
every newspaper and on every television bulletin. It was the
blank expression on the face of the England midfield player,
Paul Ince. What was going on inside his head? Did it occur
to him somewhere at the back of his skull that he might be
partly responsible for the mayhem in the stands? Did he see
any connection between the behaviour of the English thugs
and his own conduct at Selhurst Park three weeks ago? That
night millions of television viewers saw Ince rush
menacingly towards the crowd after his Manchester United
colleague Cantona had executed his notorious drop kick on
a Crystal Palace supporter. Ince is alleged to have screamed:
'Come on then, we'll take you all,' and assaulted a Palace
supporter. At the time of the international he was on police
bail after being interviewed by detectives. His demeanour
at Selhurst Park was hardly calculated to bring the game
into repute. Yet no action has been taken against him by his
club and in Dublin he was allowed to pull on an England
shirt.

The police themselves seemed reluctant to get involved,
even though the incident happened in front of their eyes and
the eyes of the television audience. It took them two weeks
to interview Ince and even then they did so by appointment.
The delay allowed Cantona to flit off to Guadeloupe after
United – in a rare and commendable pre-emptive strike –
suspended him for the rest of the season. Had Ince and

Cantona been members of the paying public they would have been hauled away by the Boys in Blue that evening and brought before the magistrates the following morning. Yet even after Ince had been bailed, a Football Association spokesman was quoted as saying that there was no reason why he should not be selected to represent his country against the Irish. 'He has not been charged and his status in the community has not changed.' I remember remarking that Rosemary West, the woman in the Gloucester House of Horror case, was innocent until proven guilty, for that matter. But I didn't hear anyone suggest she should be allowed to run a Brownie Pack until her case came to trial. The usual pundits and apologists were trotting out their predictable 'it's not a football problem, it's society's problem' excuses in the wake of the thuggery in Dublin. It might be society's problem, but it is first and foremost football's problem. There was none of this nonsense at the rugby international at Landsdowne Road a couple of weeks earlier.

Just a month before the Chelsea fans rioted in Dublin, Dennis Wise, the captain of Chelsea, was convicted of beating up a taxi driver and smashing his cab window. It is his second conviction for criminal damage. Was this highly paid role model disciplined by his club? Was he stripped of the captaincy? Er, no. 'It is not a football-related matter,' said Chelsea chairman Ken Bates. The Saturday after the court case, Wise was back in the side and dancing on the pitch with a fan after scoring the equaliser against Spurs – the same pitch which a couple of days earlier had been carpeted with mounted police attempting to break up fighting between Chelsea and Millwall fans. I suppose that wasn't a football-related matter, either. After all, the pitch invasion didn't happen until after the final whistle had blown.

Don't the self-important nonentities who run the FA see any connection whatsoever between their attitude towards violent, moronic players and the behaviour of violent, moronic supporters? The lame response of the police to the Selhurst Park affair was another contributory factor. So was the reaction of the 'Cantona is Innocent' brigade. He was provoked, wassne? Even the thickest skinhead is capable of reasoning that what's permissible for the highest-paid players in the land is perfectly permissible for him, too. Hardly surprising then that United fans continued to chant Cantona's name, even after he disappeared on holiday to Guadeloupe to escape police questioning. These are the same people who will go out and spend £70 on a garish blue and white United shirt even though they haven't got a pot to piss in and are probably signing on the social. Some of the newspapers even featured a picture of a young boy – who couldn't have been more than about six – going into Old Trafford with 'Cantona Is Innocent' painted on his face by his father. What hope is there? The more I think about it, the more I come to the conclusion that we get the footballers we deserve.

HOSPITALS FOR HYPOCHONDRIACS

Don't laugh. It had to happen. A hospital for hypochondriacs is to open in Norway. 'Hypochondriacs may only imagine they are ill, but they really do suffer,' said Dr Ingvard Wilhelmen, the man in charge of the project. 'When they have a headache they are convinced they have a brain tumour.' To which the proper medical response should be to advise them to take a couple of Panadols and pull themselves together, not to admit them to hospital. I can only suppose the Norwegians are even more soppy than we are and have even more money to waste on their version of the NHS.

Once news of the development reaches Britain it will take on a life of its own. National Hypochondria Week is no doubt already being planned. It won't be long before an entire hypochondria industry is spawned. You can even kick it off yourself, if you'd like. This is how you go about it: First you call yourself the president of the National Hypochondria Trust and get yourself some letterheads printed. Then apply for a grant from your local authority. It should only take a few weeks to come through, especially if you say in the letter that you are particularly interested in representing gay and lesbian, non-smoking, disabled hypochondriacs drawn from the ethnic minorities. It doesn't matter if this organisation consists of nothing but you and your cat and operates from a bedsit above a kebab shop. No one will ever ask. It won't be long before you're being quoted in the local papers and on a local radio. An enterprising freelance with an eye for the main chance will befriend you and start getting your press releases in the medical press and, with any luck, the nationals. The *Guardian* and the *Independent* are your best bet – they're absolute suckers for any health story which implies that the Government is not allocating sufficient 'resources' to the problem. Soon you will be invited on to the 'Today' programme on Radio 4 and you can tell Peter Hobday that unless the Government spends another £20 billion on an army of hypochondria outreach co-ordinators, a nation-wide advertising campaign and 200 new dedicated hypo-chondria hospitals, everyone in Britain will be dead by the year 2000.

Don't worry. You won't get found out, honest. A man from NALGO and a woman from the Labour Party will back you up. They'll even make up some figures of their own. With any luck, Virginia Bottomley will be trotted out and given a hard time about callous government 'cuts' and their effect on hypochondriacs. She will read out a set of statistics which purport to show that Britain has the lowest incidence of hypochrondria in Europe. (These figures will have been made up in the back of the car on the way to the studio.) However, she will add, the Government is deeply sympathetic to the difficulties experienced by hypochon-driacs and she plans to ask the Treasury for more 'resources' to target the epidemic during the next spending round.

Trebles all round, a pat on the back for Virginia from the spin–doctors and you've got a result. Lovely jubbly. Soon adverts will start appearing for hypochrondria outreach co–ordinators on thirty grand a year and a Mondeo. There will be television documentaries and twelve-page magazine spreads warning that we are all at risk. Malingerers will limp along to demonstrations outside the House of Commons, complaining about their backs and pretending to cough and sneeze over MPs voting in the third reading of the Hypochondria Discrimination Bill, which will make it illegal to discriminate against anyone on the grounds of permanent, self-certified absenteeism, and forcing employers to provide darkened rooms – at a cost of several billion pounds – for all staff who fancy a lie-down on account of their headaches.

WHAT JUSTICE?

That British justice is a sick joke is beyond argument. Every week the courts hand down ludicrous sentences. The full weight of the criminal justice system is reserved for those who snap and take the law into their own hands. We keep being told that we must not condone vigilantism. But I find it increasingly difficult to condemn. The simple fact of the matter is that the law does not belong to judges or the police or the politicians. It belongs to all of us. We entrust the politicians to make sensible laws and employ the police and judges to enforce it. When they fail, I would argue, we are entitled to seek our own redress.

Over the past few years, out of the thousands of miscarriages of justice which have been reported in the newspapers, three have stood out to my mind. I am haunted by them. They help to explain everything which is rotten about the way the criminal justice system now operates in favour of thugs and vermin and against decent law-abiding folk. Consider first the case of Joseph Elliott. The facts are simple. One night Elliott blew his social security on drink and drugs before embarking on a spree of criminal damage with a knife. Mr Robert Osborne, a musician, discovered Elliott vandalising his car. Arming himself with a mallet from his toolkit he ran into the street to confront him. Elliott stabbed him in the heart, then kicked him for good measure as he lay bleeding to death. As Mr Osborne's wife, Diane, went to her husband's assistance, Elliott threatened her: 'I'll do you like I've just done your old man.' In court, however, he claimed that he was only acting in self-defence. And he managed to convince a jury of his innocence. He was not found guilty of murder, he was not found guilty of manslaughter. He walked out of the Old Bailey, punched the air and cheered because he was not found guilty of anything at all.

What the jury did not know, because this is the way the system works, is that this was not the first time Elliott had been in trouble with the law – he had a string of previous convictions. This was not the blameless youth defending himself against an unprovoked attack from an older man, as his defence had pretended. He had, after all, gone out armed with a knife and used it to slash car tyres – not a weapon which just happened to be lying around. This was no unfortunate accident. Mr Osborne was, admittedly, carrying a wooden mallet when he confronted Elliott. The law says he was wrong. I don't agree. Whatever the law says, he should have been entitled to protect himself against a criminal he had every reason to believe was armed with a knife. Perhaps Mr Osborne was unwise to give chase and should have called the police instead. But he had every reason to believe that the police would not bother to turn up. They had repeatedly failed to prevent attacks on cars in his neighbourhood. All the evidence suggests that police have given up trying to catch thugs like Elliott, and instead concentrate not on those who slash car tyres but on harassing motorists on the off-chance that their tyres may not meet EC tread-depth standards. In the case of Joseph Elliott, the law had already failed us even before he killed Mr Osborne.

We are entitled to ask exactly what Elliott was doing

loose on the streets to commit more crime? With his previous convictions for burglary, vandalism and violence he should have been locked away, not sent to a probation officer to have his tummy tickled and given state hand-outs to buy booze, LSD and knives. In this case, even if the police and the prosecution service thought they could not make a murder charge stick we are entitled to ask why he was not charged with a number of other offences, for instance, with being under the influence of drink and drugs? There would have been no problem making that stick. In court he admitted it. It was part of his defence. Why, also, was he not charged with criminal damage? He didn't ever deny that. He admitted slashing the car too. He said he thought it was 'funny'. Ha, bloody ha. He could have been charged with possession of an offensive weapon. He didn't deny that, either. He could have been charged with kicking Mr Osborne as he lay bleeding on the ground. Or does kicking a dying man now count as the use of 'reasonable force' in self-defence? He could at least have been charged with threatening behaviour. There must have been something which could have been made to stick and which could have removed him from society. Instead he has been freed to return to a flat 300 yards away from the home of the widow of the man he killed.

It is also worth considering what might have happened if Robert Osborne had managed to overpower and disarm Elliott and had held him hostage for twenty minutes until he coughed up his name and address or until the police arrived. If other cases are anything to go by, the police would have arrested Mr Osborne and charged him with taking the law into his own hands. Because the law can't abide any criticism, any suggestion that policemen and judges aren't doing their jobs properly. Oh dear me, no. And heaven help anyone who dares criticise a judge in his own court. Take the case of Melvyn Sollors, whose son was forced off the road by a couple of thugs and beaten with an iron bar. It took two years for the case to come to court, two years of worry and anxiety, two years in which the assault weighed heavily on the minds of the Sollors family. The stress undoubtedly accelerated the spread of Mr Sollors' cancer. But when the case did eventually come to court, the thugs were let off with a slapped wrist. They were given 150 hours of community service. Mr Sollors quite rightly felt he had been betrayed. He sought his revenge. After seeing the men who attacked his son and put him in intensive care set free by his Honour Judge Richard Raymond Buxton Cole, Mr Sollors snapped. Two years of stress, worry and frustration boiled to the surface. In the court foyer, he saw the two thugs chuckling at their pathetic sentence as they made their way out of the court, probably heading for the pub to celebrate their luck. Mr Sollors attacked them, knocked one out and had to be dragged off by court officials. He was hauled back into court and charged with contempt. The judge sent him to prison for three months after he refused to apologise. 'You should be apologising to me,' Mr Sollors told the judge. Mr Sollors, who was suffering from stomach cancer and had had three heart attacks, faced at least six weeks in jail while two violent criminals enjoyed their liberty. His early release was secured by a newspaper campaign, in which I was proud to have played a prominent part. I was deluged with letters from outraged readers. Callers to my LBC radio phone-in show jammed the switchboards to register their disgust. Mr Sollors himself wrote from prison to say how much he had been heartened by the support he had received from the Press and from ordinary, decent citizens sickened to the gut by the way in which he had been treated by a warped criminal justice system. I can remember writing at the time that there were days when I feel ashamed to be British. The day Mel Sollors was sent to prison was one of them. If any case indicated most graphically the disease at the heart of British justice it was this. Again and again the law has shown concern for the criminal and disdain for the victim. What sort of society sends a dying man to jail while the animals who put his son in hospital are let off virtually scot-free? Judges and policemen need to be reminded that the law doesn't belong to them. They are merely paid employees, charged with dispensing justice on our behalf. In that respect they are no different from the mechanics we hire to mend our cars and the decorators we hire to paint our houses. They work for us – we tell them what to do on our behalf. That is the bargain. That is the deal. No more. No less. God knows what was going on inside the thick skull under the wig of the judge in the Sollors case. Because the law does not require judges to explain their decisions we shall never know why the judge thought community service an appropriate punishment for a vicious, un-provoked assault, first with two motor vehicles and then with an iron bar.

It is sentences like this which turn people into vigilantes. And who can blame them if they then decide to cut out the middleman and dispense their own justice? It is the kind of sentences handed down by judges like Cole which send decent men berserk. And the kind of sentences handed down by judges like Mr Justice Hutchinson which encourage thugs to laugh at the law. He was the judge in the case of grandfather John Taylor, who was kicked to death by a gang of yobs on a summer's evening in a sleepy English village. Mr Taylor had been enjoying a quiet family barbecue when, at about 10.30pm, the peace was disturbed by a bunch of drunken, foul-mouthed hooligans rampaging down the street, urinating in gardens, smashing trees and vandalising parked cars. Mr Taylor and his son-in-law Robert Allan left the party to remonstrate with the mob. He politely asked them to behave themselves. Their response was to swear at him and start kicking down his fence. When he tried to stop them, he was punched to the ground. His head hit the road with such a crack that the noise was heard by people standing some distance away. The eight thugs set upon Mr Taylor and Mr Allan like a pack of dogs. Mr Allan rolled himself into a ball as they put the boot in. Mr Taylor suffered a fractured skull and died hours later without regaining consciousness. Mr Allan had to stay in hospital for three days to recover from his injuries. Some of the defendants, all aged either seventeen or eighteen, had drunk up to fifteen cans of lager, chased down by a bottle of Pernod. Phillip Hill, who threw the fatal punch, was sentenced to two and a half years after admitting man-slaughter. The others got just nine months each in a young offenders' institution when they came before Mr Justice Hutchinson at Winchester Crown Court. The judge told Hill: 'When in your drunken and boorish condition you struck that blow, you had no intent to kill or cause serious harm. Death was the unhappy and unlooked-for conse-quence of a momentry loss of temper on your part.' Turning to the others, Mr Justice Hutchinson said: 'You are all ordinary, decent young men. This is a catastrophe for your lives.' Hardly surprising that these hooligans were seen leaving the court smirking.

From reports of the case, Phillip Hill had been in a fairly bad temper for some time before he encountered Mr Taylor. He had been drinking himself into a fury and was part of a mob which had been committing criminal damage and making threats to passers-by. Death may not have been his intention, but one can argue that it was bound to be a possible consequence of his violent, moronic behaviour. As for whether or not these were all 'decent' young men: Decent young men do not drink fifteen cans of lager and a bottle of Pernod. Decent young men do not urinate in other people's gardens. Decent young men do not smash up parked cars and rip at trees like crazed orang-utans. Decent young men do not swear and make threats at civilised people going about their business. Decent young men do not kick down garden fences. Decent young men do not rampage through quiet villages at 10.30pm. Decent young men do not fall upon others like a pack of wild animals. Decent young men do not smirk when they leave a court in which they are being tried for an affray which has left one man dead and another seriously injured. Decent young men who find themselves in the dock because of a rush of blood or a momentary bout of foolishness show some respect. They dress in shirt and tie and a jacket and hang their heads in shame. They do not turn up to court in sawn-off baggies, T-shirts, designer jeans and training shoes. These were quite clearly not decent young men, as you and I understand the expression. I might have been able to go along with Mr Justice Hutchinson had they really shown the 'genuine remorse' referred to by counsel for the defence – and when I say genuine remorse, I do not mean the sort of stage remorse we see in courts up and down the land every week in the hope of conning daft judges into passing lenient sentences.

A public statement from the young men or their families expressing sincere apologies might have been in order. Something like: 'Whatever sentence we have been given, it can never make up for the loss of a husband, a father and grandfather.' Perhaps even an offer to pay part of their wages every week, once they were released, to Mr Taylor's widow and dependants for the loss of a breadwinner. A bunch of flowers to Mrs Taylor might have been the sort of gesture decent young men and their decent parents would have made. Instead, a judge gave them the kind of sentence which will have thugs like them laughing into their lager tops in Karaoke bars all over Britain.

Tory MP Peter Viggers, whose constituency includes the Taylor family home in Alverstoke, Hampshire, said: 'This was a disgusting and inexcusable act of violence and I would have expected the sentence to reflect this. I am ashamed to be part of a society that allows this kind of conduct.' You and me both, Mr Viggers.

Until fairly recently I have been opposed to the American system of electing judges and police chiefs. But I am now convinced that the only way to make the forces of law and order properly accountable to those of us who pay their wages is to make them face the electorate at least every two years. Then instead of policing in a way which they find most convenient and least threatening to themselves, instead of bullying motorists, they might actually get around to keeping the peace. I would also make the office of public prosecutor subject to regular election. That would mean fewer politically correct prosecutions and more effort put into securing conviction against muggers, burglars, vandals and violent offenders. Judges, too, would have to account for their actions and explain their sentencing policy. That way you simply wouldn't get the kind of miscarriages of justice discussed in this chapter and the law would work in favour of decent, law-abiding people such as Melvyn Sollors and against thugs like Joseph Elliott and those who kicked John Taylor to death on a quiet English summer's evening.

GIMME, GIMME, GIMME

When I presented my first television programme on LWT, 'Richard Littlejohn, Live and Uncut', I found myself lined up against an array of ghastly professional lesbians. I was arguing rationally and reasonably that it was not the business of the NHS to provide artificial insemination for women who can't even abide the thought of becoming pregnant in the natural manner.

I also ventured the revolutionary opinion that in an ideal world all children needed both a male and a female parent. I was on a hiding to nothing. Even one of my guests for the evening, the delightful and robustly heterosexual mother, Nigella Lawson, *Times* and *Spectator* columnist, described my positon as 'extreme'. Michael Winner, the film director, put it even more bluntly. He called me an 'arsehole'.

Let me state, just for the record, that I have absolutely nothing against lesbians. They are free to do whatever they wish. But I simply can't see why it should be subsidised by the British taxpayer. The debate was sparked by the decision of Leicester Royal Infirmary to offer fertility treatment to two lesbian couples. Health Secretary Virginia Bottomley was greeted with howls of derision when she said she proposed tightening up the rules to prevent this happening. She was accused of discrimination and sexism. No force on earth can prevent a lesbian getting pregnant if she so wishes and can find a willing male partner to inseminate her either naturally or artificially. But the National Health Service does not exist to give lesbians babies on demand. Fertility treatment is complex and expensive and designed to give heterosexual couples one last chance at parenthood when all else has failed. Once this service was offered there was a queue of lesbians demanding to be impregnated and announcing their 'right' to bring up children on welfare benefit.

In Manchester, two lesbians living on state benefits were legally recognised by the High Court as parents of a child conceived – less than immaculately it is fair to assume – by one of them after a perfunctory exchange of body fluids with a male friend. We were not allowed to know their identities even though we are paying for all this, not only through the dole but via legal aid. One of the women involved already had two other children. After six weeks together they decided they wanted a child of 'their own'. Forget the biological difficulties for a moment. Both these women are unemployed, receiving single person's benefit. It is reckless and selfish – even for a heterosexual couple – to bring another child into the world in those circumstances and expect other people to finance it. The legal aid system, which is already horrendously expensive, was intended to ensure that everyone could have a proper defence – not to fund absurd test cases such as this.

It is yet another example of the cancer of political correctness being spread by public expenditure. As I acknowledged earlier, no force on earth could have prevented this baby if the woman was so minded. But it should not have been made such an attractive proposition by the state. As for the father, he said he had no intention of having anything to do with the fruit of his loins. As far as he was concerned, his part in the whole affair went no further than a test-tube and a copy of *Penthouse*. He then had the cheek to complain that the Child Support Agency was hounding him for maintenance. His complaint was that he couldn't afford any payment because he was unemployed. In which case he shouldn't have been fathering any child, either naturally or artificially. It is only a pity the law does not permit compulsory vasectomy – or, better, castration – as well as an attachment-of-earnings order.

Mind you, it's hardly surprising that these dykes are demanding babies when the world's highest-profile lesbian, tennis star Martina Navratilova, announced her intention to become a mum by a sperm donor. Somehow the notion has got around that every woman has the 'right' to a baby even if she finds the idea of indulging in a few moments of natural reproductive activity utterly repellent. There is a world of difference though between Miss Navratilova, who can afford to support a child without the assistance of a natural father, and Miss Becky Grady, from Coventry. Unemployed lesbian Miss Grady was not as reticent as the Manchester women who wanted to keep their identities secret from the rest of us, even though we were funding their bizarre lifestyle. She was more than happy to be photographed with her son, born after treatment at a clinic recommended by London's gay switchboard.

If you were ever in any doubt that the world has gone stark, staring bonkers, I invite you to consider what Miss Grady had to say. She openly boasted of her intention to bring up her son, Jack, on welfare. 'Jack won't have a father, but that's not important. I wanted a baby, lots of lesbians do. And if that's what they want then they should be allowed treatment on the NHS. I get enough income support for both of us.' So that's all right then. Miss Grady made it clear she could not stomach the idea of conceiving in the normal way. 'Sleeping with a man would be for me like asking a straight woman to sleep with another woman. I don't think the gay switchboard thought my case was unusual.' I'm sure it didn't. Yet another example of the Gimme, Gimme, Gimme society. Snap your fingers and the state will provide. We are all going to hell in a handcart.

Still, there's always a funny side. This being my first ever TV show, I was particularly concerned that the audience should be in the right frame of mind. My agent advised me to make a point of thanking the warm-up man. He can make or break the first five minutes of any show. Now my experience of warm-up men has been that they tend to be Redcoat types in Supermarket Sweep jackets. About ten minutes before we were due on air outside the studio I spotted a guy in a bright red jacket, walked up to him and thanked him profusely for all his help. 'I can't tell you how important your contribution is to me, old boy. Just one thing, though – we've got a roomful of dykes in tonight, so go easy on the shirtlifter gags.'

When I walked into the studio and sat behind my desk, I realised that he wasn't the warm-up man after all. There was a completely different comic out there. Who the hell was the bloke I had chatted to earlier, then? My eyes scanned the studio. There in the second row, scowling at me, was chummy in the red jacket. I hastily looked at the seating plan on the desk in front of me. It turned out that far from him being a comic, he was in fact the deputy chairman of the Lambeth Campaign for Homosexual Equality! I spent the first thirty minutes ignoring his attempts to get in on the argument. Come the interval he climbed out of his seat and rushed the stage. He was ushered away by my producers, who were completely oblivious of the reason for his grievance.

The following week, as I was talking to Ken Livingstone

and club owner Peter Stringfellow, the show was interrupted by pictures transmitted in error from a satellite feed. The interruption featured a steamy lesbian sex scene. No one would believe it wasn't deliberate.

You couldn't make it up, could you?

CITY OF SELF-PITY

In the wake of the James Bulger murder trial came the most extraordinary statement from Liverpool City Council. It stressed that the case had 'no feature particular to Liverpool' and called on the media to show 'sensitivity and restraint'. This hideous crime could have been committed in any city in Britain, but you wouldn't have seen a similar eleven-paragraph, 375-word statement from councillors in Birmingham or Tunbridge Wells. No one had actually pointed the finger at Liverpool as a whole. They wouldn't dare. It is politically incorrect to do so. Even the mildest criticism of the city provokes an hysterical over-reaction. This is a mawkish city with a chip on both shoulders. The council's statement was an attempt to get its retaliation in first. We're warning you, pal. One word, just one word. That's all. Are you looking at me? Everyone thinks Harry Enfield's stroppy, scrapping Scousers are a caricature. I keep telling you – you couldn't make it up.

Because of this emotional and commercial blackmail, newspapers didn't even attempt to investigate whether there might be any aspect of the case peculiar to Liverpool. But there were aspects which – while they do apply elsewhere – had the Mersey trademark stamped all over them. There were the good things, like the old-fashioned sense of community, the rallying round in time of adversity. Then there are the less savoury aspects – the automatic tendency to blame everything on someone else, the refusal to accept responsibility, the wallowing in self-pity, the acceptance of petty crime as a way of life. Liverpool is the only city where you will hear the word 'scally' – an affectionate term for a juvenile delinquent.

This was the reaction of Mrs Anne Thompson, mother of one of the boys who killed James Bulger: 'He's a little liar, he's devious, he's a scally, he robs, he plays truant, it's his hobby. He's not a murderer. He swears blind he hasn't done it and I believe him.' So that's all right then. Off down the chippie and get yerself a bag of chips for your dinner, you cheeky beggar. And bring me back twenty Bensons.

I do not know Mrs Thompson. What we did discover at the time was that she had seven children by two different fathers, neither of whom lived with her. She accepted no responsibility for what happened, preferring to blame social workers, teachers, police officers, in fact anyone but herself. She is a living, swearing example of all that is rotten about the dependency culture this country has spawned over the past thirty years. There are, of course, Anne Thompsons all over the country. But Liverpool is perhaps the only place where she would receive widespread sympathy.

There was another image of this case which sticks in my memory to this day. It is of grown men and women – many of them in lurid shellsuits – their faces contorted in hate, screaming, scratching and tearing at the police van they thought contained the two boys. In fact, it didn't. But what if it had? What would they have done if they had got at these pre-pubescent children? Would they have torn them limb from limb or strung them up from the nearest lamp-post? Here was a community turning in upon itself. They knew it could have been their son or daughter lying dead and mutilated on that railway line.

There are other cities with similar social problems. There are other estates where parents collect their dole, buy their Special Brew and ciggies, rent *Child's Play 3* and slump on the sofa in front of Anne and Nick, not giving a bugger what the children they brought into the world are up to. Large parts of the country have gone down the toilet. It is not just the fault of the government, the folk who live here must share the blame. They have obviously never heard the advice about not shitting on your own doorstep. These are people who shit on their own doormat, as well as their neighbour's. There is ignorance, moral decay and rampant crime. Sure, there may be few jobs. But if there were, an awful lot of these people would still be unemployable.

At the risk of sounding like a Tory backwoodsman, perhaps this crime might have been prevented if Mrs Thompson had only two children and had brought them up in a stable, two-parent relationship. Instead she thinks she can go on breeding like a rabbit and expecting the state to clear up her mess. If ever there was a case for compulsory sterilisation, she is it.

No matter how shocking what happened to James Bulger was, I am only surprised it doesn't happen more often. There are too many parents – all over Britain – who don't care where their children are at any given hour of the day or night, who they mix with or what they watch. Most are happy to trot off to the boozer, leaving youngsters gaping at *Driller Killer* on the flickering blue parent in the corner. These are the same people who keep dogs called Tyson and let them roam free. And when Tyson rips the throat out of a toddler, they say it was the child's fault for provoking him, he wouldn't hurt a fly. They are, quite frankly, low life. The scum of the earth. And giving them money and social workers and encouraging them to believe that they needn't take responsibility for anything only makes it worse.

This doesn't only apply to Liverpool. It is a nationwide problem which can't be swept under the carpet. It must be addressed, even if it means having to swallow unpalatable truths. After the two boys were found guilty of murdering James Bulger, we had to listen to a conga line of experts blaming everyone and everything from the social services and unemployment to bingo to killer videos. There is no simple answer. There may not even be any answer at all. But until the likes of Liverpool City Council stop issuing irrelevant, self-obsessed press releases and face facts, there never will be.

TIE A YELLOW RIBBON

Those little red AIDS ribbons being sported by assorted pop singers, politicians and luvvies and pressed upon guests at awards ceremonies stick in my craw. They even make metal AIDS ribbons and I've seen ostentatious jewelled versions – which is about as tasteless as you can get.

Now everyone is getting in on the act. Tony Banks, the Labour MP for Newham, turned up on my Sky TV show wearing a purple ribbon. 'What's that for?' I asked. 'VD?'

'No,' he explained. 'Veal calves.'

Apparently there are all sorts of different coloured ribbons for all manner of causes. Those of us who have had our fill of this absurd posturing should find a symbol of our own, to be worn on the lapel at all times, to demonstrate our displeasure. A miniature noose might do the trick.

ORANGES AREN'T THE ONLY FRUITS

Just when the Tories thought things couldn't get any worse, Steven Milligan, MP for Eastleigh, Hants, was found dead in unusual circumstances. In my *Sun* column I observed: 'There's a scene in the movie *The Long Good Friday* in which Bob Hoskins is trying to cover up a murder by removing the corpse in an ice-cream van. "Not very dignified, is it?" remarks Hoskins, as the gang boss Harold Shand, "going out like a raspberry ripple." Nor is it very dignified going out like an oven-ready, boil-in-the bag duck *à l'orange*,' I added. Mr Milligan, you may recall, was discovered on his kitchen table trussed up with electrical flex, dressed only in women's stockings. His head was in a black plastic bin-liner, there was a noose around his neck and a satsuma in his mouth.

As a junior reporter, I covered some unusual inquests in which men – it was always men – had died in similar bizarre circumstances. Men hanging from rafters dressed as frog-men. Men who had tied nooses around their necks, tethered the cable to their ankles, inserted themselves into cylindrical vacuum cleaners and bid a fond farewell to the world when they turned the suction on full. Each to their own, I suppose. If that's what turns them on. Mr Milligan was a single man and what he got up to in the privacy of his own kitchen was entirely a matter for him – although I'd have thought dicing with death in pursuit of a momentary shudder and 10cc of salty emission was a little irresponsible in a man elected to serve 60,000 constituents and tipped as a future Prime Minister.

What puzzles me is what might have happened if the doorbell had rung half-way through. Presumably Mr Milligan had passed many a quiet evening at home in a similar fashion. What if he had ordered a pizza and forgotten about it? Or the Jehovah's Witnesses had called? How would he have answered the door? Or if a neighbour had called to borrow a cup of sugar? Exactly how do you talk your way out of that? There is another aspect which baffles me, too. Who thought it up in the first place? I mean, imagine you are sitting at home of an evening a bit bored. There's nothing much on the TV, the video shop's shut, you've read the papers and can't be bothered going to the pub. I know, you think to yourself, I'll make my own entertainment, just like people used to do in the good old days. So you rummage around the house to see what you can find. You come across a length of electrical flex and a plastic bin-liner. You could do a number of things. You could make a kite, or a glove puppet. You've got one orange left. You could hang the bin-liner on the wall, cut the bottom out and play basketball. You could use the flex to make a sling. The possibilities are endless. But it's a bit warm in the house and the suit you wore for work is making you a bit sweaty. Time to slip into something more comfortable, you think. Then you remember you've got a pair of women's stockings in the bottom drawer. You strip naked and glide them over your hairy calves. Now what? I am assuming at this stage that you don't possess a mirror. It would be impossible to look in it without laughing. Eureka! By George, I think I've got it! You stick the satsuma in your mouth, pull the bin-liner over your head, tie you legs and arms together, put a noose round your neck and wriggle on the pine table. Why didn't I think of this before? And if you get out of it alive, you have an overwhelming desire to tell a friend and spread the gospel. Sure beats the hell out of solitaire.

Call me old-fashioned, but if this was how I spent my evenings I'd want to keep pretty quiet about it. Yet in the wake of the Milligan affair we were reliably told that this was pretty routine behaviour in certain circles. So, apparently, is something called felching. It was not a word with which I was familiar until someone explained to me the origin of the expression Pet Shop Boys, which has been adopted by a successful British pop group. Felching, yet again, seems to be an exclusively male pursuit. It is not something your average West End Girl is likely to take part in. It involves, in technical terms, shoving a live gerbil up your arse, and is particularly popular in some circles – allegedly numbering at least one Hollywood celebrity amongst its aficionados. There are, I am led to believe, a couple of variations on this particular theme. The first involves a gerbil and a polythene bag, the second a shaved gerbil liberally sprinkled with cocaine.

At this stage, I think a discreet veil is called for. But, again, I would like to meet the man who first thought of it. And where, exactly, do you get the gerbils from? Imagine, just for a moment, you are a pet shop owner. A moustachioed, cropped-haired man in one-size-too-small shrink-to-fit Levi 501s and a lumbercheck shirt comes in and asks to buy a gerbil. This is all he wants. He showed no interest in gerbil food, or a little gerbil collar, and resists your attempts to sell him a gerbil cage and a little gerbil exercise wheel. This might suggest to you that he has no long-term plans for the gerbil. He also asks if there is any discount for buying in bulk, say half a dozen, or laying a regular weekly order and, by the way, do you do home delivery – and if you do, can you bring them round in a polythene bag and push them through the letter-box if he's not there? But be careful, because he wants them alive and scratching. Oh, and as an afterthought, he asks if there is anywhere around here he can buy a little razor – a Ladyshave, perhaps. Do you sell him what he wants, or do you call the RSPCA? Or the YMCA? It's a dilemma, isn't it? Maybe they get them mail order. Me, I'd rather have a raspberry ripple.

Warning from the Government Chief Medical Officers: The practices discussed in this chapter could be hazardous to your health. You are not advised to try them at home.

PRETTY PARROT

They say you should never work with children and animals. They are not making it up. I can still vividly remember the 'Blue Peter' elephant dumping ordure all over the studio as Auntie Val Singleton, Uncle Chris Trace and Cousin John Noakes ran for cover. Every actor has a horror story about trying to perform alongside an animal. To children and animals, add birds.

On my penultimate Sky television show of 1994, we had planned to cross live to the dressing room of the Mermaid Theatre in London to talk to the actor Roy Marsden, of TV's Inspector Dalgleish fame, starring as Long John Silver in the traditional Christmas production of *Treasure Island*, a role made famous by the late Sir Bernard Miles. The plan was also to talk to Marsden's co-star, a parrot called Arnie. I can remember asking in advance if this was wise. I was assured that all would be well. Arnie was used to the lights and was reliably house-trained. He had already been interviewed by a number of newspapers. The way it works is this: the camera crew turn up at the theatre and set up a live link. The interviewee talks to the camera, I talk to a TV screen set up at the end of my desk in the studio. The line goes live during the 6.30 news headlines, which come from Sky's headquarters at Osterley, in West London. This gives us a couple of minutes to make sure everything is working properly. During this time, I can see what is going on at the other end but can't speak to the subject of the interview. All I could see on my screen was Roy Marsden, in full costume. No Arnie.

'Where's Arnie?' I asked my producer.

'I'm afraid Arnie can't be with us tonight,' came the reply.

'Why not?'

'Arnie is no longer with the show.'

'But it doesn't open officially until tonight,' I said.

'That is technically true.'

'So what happened?'

'Arnie has been sacked.'

'Why?'

'This afternoon, he told 600 schoolchildren to fuck off.'

MR PLOD HAS LOST THE PLOT

When it comes to the police, you really can't make it up. A correspondent wrote to Her Majesty's *Daily Telegraph* suggesting that, to relieve their boredom, traffic police could play a form of snooker – 'potting' cars in order of colour. One point for red, two for yellow and so on, just like the real thing. Unfortunately, the constabulary had got there first. A couple of months earlier, the *Sun* reported that patrolmen in Essex were playing 'motorway snooker' on the M11. Except they reversed the pink and black to make it more difficult. Imagine a typical day's work for Z-Victor One, cruising the black stuff between Harlow and the Stansted airport turn-off.

'Oi, George, did you see that Porsche? He must have been doing at least 150 miles an hour. Come on, let's nick him.'

'Sorry, Bill. We can't go after him.'

'Why not?'

'How many times have I got to tell you that you can't go after a colour until you've potted a red? The Porsche is black.'

'But he's breaking the law, George.'

'So is just about everyone else on this motorway, Bill. That's not the point. We've got the final coming up against the Cambridgeshire traffic police next week. If we don't get our scores up, we won't even make the squad?'

'The Flying Squad?'

'Don't be so bloody silly, Bill. The *snooker* squad.'

'Oh, right, George, gotcha.'

'Look, here comes one now.'

'I can see it – red Metro.'

'Precisely.'

'But the radar is only registering 68mph.'

'We'll have to think of something else.'

'Such as?'

'I dunno, be inventive. Use your initiative – drunken driving, random tax disc check. Anything will do.'

'But it's a vicar behind the wheel.'

'Well then, stands to reason, dunnit?'

'What stands to reason?'

'He's bound to be pissed, innee?'

'Why?'

'Communion wine. Drink it by the gallon, these clerics. Let's get after him.'

'But he's driving perfectly safely.'

'No one ever drives perfectly safely. A car's a lethal weapon, innit? He's bound to be doing something wrong.'

'Fair enough. Let's go. The sooner we nick him, the sooner we can start building up a score. Where did that Porsche go? No one's ever got a maximum 147 break on this stretch.'

If you think it's nonsense to suggest that the Old Bill go in for keeping score on the motorways, then consider this memorandum to all patrol officers in Kent. It was sent by Inspector R. Bartlett, area traffic inspector responsible for policing the M2, M20 and part of the M25. It read as follows:

> There will be a minimum standard by which patrols are to be measured. They are expected to submit

> process against one defendant for each day of the
> month worked, i.e. normally twenty days worked,
> twenty defendants. The spread of activity will be at
> least five FPTs, five VDRs and five Summons/Charge
> Reports and advises should be at a level of at least two
> per day . . . Any patrol not achieving the standard set
> will be spoken to by his Section Sergeant . . . Patrols
> who consistently fail to meet the standard will have to
> seriously consider their future on Traffic.
>
> Area Traffic Inspector

In other words, if you don't nick enough motorists you will
be out on your arse. It is worth pointing out that when this
memo was issued, Kent had been suffering from a record
number of burglaries – especially in the area immediately
adjacent to the motorway network. For instance, 'The
Darling Buds of May' village of Pluckley and its neighbouring village of Charing have been plagued by crime,
suffering sixty-one burglaries in eighteen months. In the
previous year in Kent as a whole there were 18,444
domestic burglaries – an increase of 16 per cent. Four out of
five were not cleared up. Village police stations were closed
as a matter of routine and often officers would have to travel
over twenty miles to respond to a 999 call. Yet the police
were issuing memos threatening traffic patrol officers with
disciplinary action if they didn't nick enough motorists. I
don't know about you, but I have never, ever heard of any
target being set for the appprehension of burglars.

The police are always pleading limited 'resources'. In
which case those 'resources' they have should be targeted
where they are most needed – in the fight against real crime.
For the price of two coppers and the purchase and running
cost of an unmarked Rover 827 Vitesse, equipped with the
very latest all-singing, all-dancing Vascar radar gear and

video recording equipment, three villages could get their bobbies back. If you asked the villagers of Pluckley and Charing what they would rather have, PC Dixon would beat CHiPs every time. But 'community' policing only applies to violent inner-city areas with large ethnic populations and stroppy local councillors.

Saturation policing of the motorways is one of the least efficient uses of police time, money and manpower. Motorway travel is the safest form of road transport in Britain. 100mph in a properly maintained modern vehicle is safer than a doddery old lady doing 27mph in an Austin A40 in a built-up area. But the police continue to resist all calls to raise the speed limit on motorways. That's because it's easy to nick someone doing 78mph in a Mondeo. The radar says so and the radar never lies. Oh, doesn't it? One of the most significant aspects of the case of a motorcyclist accused of travelling at 178mph on the M6 was the proven inaccuracy of the radar/video device which registered his speed. The motorcyclist was fined and banned from driving, but not until after the magistrates accepted expert witness evidence that the machine he was riding had been extensively tested and it had been proved beyond doubt that it was incapable of travelling at more than 160mph. This doesn't mean that the case should have been thrown out of court, but it does prove that radar can lie. And if one machine shows a man who couldn't possibly have been exceeding 160mph doing 178mph – an inaccuracy of more than 10 per cent – then how many other people nicked for speeding much nearer the limit have been wrongly convicted? I only ask, because when the case came to court in February 1995, no one appeared to pick up on it. And with spy cameras being fitted on roads all over the country, perhaps we should question the technology. As someone who has worked on newspapers all his life, I can assure you: the camera often lies.

Who is to say that the speed-trap cameras have been properly calibrated? Would you let a copper set your video? I rest my case, your honour. But we bovinely accept any radar or camera evidence shown to us, just like a dopey shop assistant who will unquestioningly accept that two boxes of matches at 20p each amount to £3,400.75 because that's how the electronic till reads the bar code. Muss be right, mussnit? (Speaking of supermarket error, when was the last time the till went wrong in the customer's favour?) Mr Plod has lost the plot completely. In some ways I can understand why, even if I can't sympathise with them or condone their attitude.

They have become so sick and tired with the system that they have given up the ghost completely. Emasculated by the politicians, betrayed by the courts and the Crown Prosecution Service, they have abandoned the fight against crime and, instead, to keep themselves busy, they take out their resentment on the rest of us. We are treated like rabble, to be bullied when they feel like it and to be ignored when we seek their assistance. These days, if you want to know the time, buy a watch.

Let me give you a couple of examples, which you may consider trivial, but illustrate what I'm getting at. When I was working at LBC Radio, whose studios are in west London, I used to have to travel every day around the Shepherd Bush one-way system near the old BBC Television Theatre. For want of anything better to do, Hammersmith and Fulham Council have decided to waste hundreds of thousands of pounds buggering it up. They moved in with their little red bricks (see elsewhere) one weekend and closed off one stretch to everything except buses – ensuring that you now have to drive half-way to Southend to get back to where you started from. On day one, there were five police officers, one motorbike, one

Panda car and a van nicking people for taking the same shortcut they had been taking for donkey's years. For months afterwards, there was a copper on full-time duty there. Later that same day, just round the corner, a friend of mine had his car window smashed and his phone stolen while he turned his back for a couple of minutes. He even saw the bloke who did it. The police took half an hour to respond to his call for help and told him there was nothing they could do. They were all too busy nicking motorists for driving in a new bus lane.

Last summer, a woman neighbour of mine who works as a doctor's receptionist was confronted by a known drug addict demanding a prescription. The woman doctor on duty refused. He wouldn't leave and became violent and offensive. There were genuine fears that he would go out and mug someone for money to buy drugs unless they gave him what he wanted. The doctor called the local nick, about half a mile away, for help. She was told there was no one available because all 'resources' were tied up policing a 'major local event'. This 'major' event turned out to be the annual carnival parade, which consists of one black cab, a milk float, a pack of Brownies and a couple of blokes banging oil drums. We are not exactly talking Notting Hill here. Eventually the druggie left quietly. But what if he had stabbed the woman to death while the Old Bill were out in force in the park watching the reggae version of 'The Birdie Song'? More 'community' policing, you see.

Over the years, my postbag has been full of similar examples, some of them from serving police officers who are disgusted at what The Job has become. A friend of mine was invited to lunch at Scotland Yard. Over the port and Stilton he was taken to one side by a very high-ranking officer. The officer was concerned about the number of critical articles I had written about the police force. Was I a communist, he wanted to know? Was I some kind of subversive? Whose side was I on? My friend, a right-wing Law and Order fetishist, supped his Cockburns and replied: 'Oh, you can take it from me – Littlejohn's on our side. The trouble is, he doesn't think *you* are on our side any more.'

In 1988 I was writing a column for the *Evening Standard* in London. I got wind of a new crime 'screening' scheme. It turned out that the Metropolitan Police had decided to award crimes a series of points, based on seriousness and the likelihood of an arrest. Any crime which rated less than three on the scale would not be followed up. For instance, a poor description of an assailant, or a burglary through an open door, would only merit one point. So would a theft from a car. This way, crimes which had no hope of being solved would be screened out. And if they weren't recorded, then, hey presto, crime would miraculously appear to fall. I covered this story in some detail, backed up by quotes from police officers disturbed at developments. Officially, I was pilloried. The police investigated every crime thoroughly, there was no question of certain crimes being screwed up and consigned to the squadroom waste-paper basket, came the outraged response from Scotland Yard and the Home Office. Privately, officers confirmed to me that I had hit the nail on the head and the Yard was simply embarrassed because all the new system had done was to institutionalise and legitimise what had been quietly going on for donkey's years.

Since then things have got even worse. Now criminals who are caught are being set free without ever coming to court under a new code, which also awards points. Within the Metropolitan Police it has been dubbed the Criminals' Charter and is contained in a forty-three-page manual. Once again outrage greeted news of the code, when it was revealed in the *Mail on Sunday* by crime correspondent

Chester Stern, himself a former Yard press officer. Under the code, each offence is given a score from one to five – sound familiar? – which measures its seriousness. This is called a disposal option. Crimes such as murder are awarded the maximum five points, which always leads to a prosecution. But other crimes – including minor burglaries, thefts of and from cars, bomb hoaxes, possession of a small amount of drugs, even rape if the 'victim' is believed to have 'consented' – are downgraded and the perpetrator allowed to walk free. No prosecution, no costly trial, no conviction, no social reports, no prison sentence, no windsurfing holiday. And best of all as far as the politicians and the chief police officers are concerned, no crime statistic. Trebles and medals all round.

Meanwhile, back on the M11, the points are accumulating. While at the nick a rapist and a burglar are walking free because they only scored three apiece, our intrepid patrolmen are on for a record break. You couldn't make it up, you really couldn't.

The other major problem facing the police force is the obsession with political correctness. Sir Paul Condon, the commissioner of the Metropolitan Police, must be a secret *Guardian* reader. Witness his directive to allow homosexual policemen to share police married quarters. Fair enough. Some of my best friends, and all that. The domestic arrangements of police officers are nobody's business but their own, provided they are not living in a crack house or shacking up with known criminals. But perversely, this concession only applies to homosexuals – and lesbians, provided they don't want to share with each other. It is an unwavering rule of political correctness that something that has the perfectly legitimate aim of eliminating discrimination against a minority always ends up discriminating against the majority. Heterosexual coppers are not allowed to live together in police accommodation. Further proof, if proof were needed, that the Old Bill is going soft on burglars. And it brings a whole new meaning to the expression 'bent copper'.

A BMW IN EVERY DRIVEWAY

According to the Rowntree Foundation's 1995 report, poverty in Britain is on the increase. It stated that since 1979, the lowest income groups had not benefited from economic growth. The report was at best misleading and proves how statistics can be manipulated for political gain. No one is suggesting that there is no poverty in this country. But what we are talking about is relative poverty rather than absolute poverty. The truth is that over the past twenty-five years disposable income – the most reliable indicator of what people have to spend after tax – has risen by almost 80 per cent for all income groups. Some people have undeniably done better than others. The government's own figures reveal that the top fifth of the population now account for 43 per cent of national income, while the bottom 10 per cent have dropped from 10 per cent to 6 per cent of the total. But there is no evidence to suggest that standards of living for those bottom 10 per cent have fallen. In fact, there is evidence to suggest that standards of living for lower income groups have improved. The proportion of the poorest tenth of the population with a telephone climbed from 47 per cent to 68 per cent. The proportion with central heating increased from 42 per cent to 70 per cent. Half the 'poor' have videos. And the report takes no account of social mobility. People move in and out of different income groups all the time. Some get richer, some get poorer. It happens. Pensioners as a group are better off than ever before in relative terms largely because of SERPS, the growth of occupational pensions and the rise in house prices. In 1979, a third of pensioners were among the poorest 10 per cent. By 1994 only one in eight fell into that category.

The Rowntree Trust trotted out the usual solutions, increase benefits and family credits. Make more people dependent on the state. That's the usual left-wing panacea. But already there are generous state provisions. There is no good reason for anyone in Britain to go without food, clothing, a roof over their head or free medical attention. We don't have real poverty any more. We don't have the raw want which characterised the 1930s. What we do have is people who are poor in relation to others. That's different. It all depends how you define poverty. There is a move from Brussels to categorise anyone on less than half average wages as living in poverty. In a feature on poverty, the *Observer* invited us to weep for an unemployed, unmarried couple with three children having to get by on £200 a week in State benefits. We were told that they lived in a three-bedroomed house and could only afford to run a battered old Vauxhall. The *Observer* contrasted them with their more affluent neighbours in Sussex who drive BMWs and kit out their kids in designer trainers. It complained that their £200 a week was 'barely enough to pay the bills' and they didn't have enough left over to pay for a holiday. Tough. We might ask why, if the male partner hasn't worked for ten years, they went on having children? We might also ask what makes them any different from the hundreds of thousands of people in low-paid jobs who manage on less than £200 a week? All over Britain families get by on that kind of money and less after tax. They don't all live in three-bedroomed houses and many of them can't afford any sort of car – let alone a battered Vauxhall. These hard-working families might consider themselves a bit hard up, but they would be insulted if they were told they are living 'in poverty', which is what the Rowntree Trust and the Labour front bench considers them to be. If they want a holiday they save up for it. They don't expect the State to cater for their every whim.

We are entitled to expect no more from the State than to ensure that people are fed, clothed and warm and have access to free health care and education for their children if, for any legitimate reason, and only for any legitimate reason, they are unable to provide for themselves. Yet somehow the idea has got around – promoted by the professional poverty industry – that everyone is entitled to wealth and happiness and video recorders at the taxpayers' expense. The poverty industry is just like the equal opportunities and race relations industries. It is completely out of control – and we are picking up the tab. A lot of highly paid officials and outreach co-ordinators are seeking out poverty where it doesn't exist in order to justify their own jobs and company cars. They have a vested interest in identifying as much 'poverty' as possible. There's a big drink in it for them. They are aided and abetted by ex-public schoolboys in corduroy suits from the BBC and the *Observer* who attempt to make us feel guilty about the feckless and the poor as penance for their own privileged backgrounds. Thus someone from a poverty charity is invited on Radio Four to demand more 'resources' to buy fancy shellsuits for the children of unmarried mothers. Unless these shellsuits are provided by the end of the week these unfortunate youngsters, already suffering from 'emotional deprivation', will be scarred for the rest of their lives, we are told as the BBC reporter chokes back the tears.

Instead of telling them to get stuffed, Tory ministers immediately go on the defensive and promise more money because they are afraid of being called 'uncaring' – and up go our taxes again to pay for it. It is not the job of the State to provide foreign holidays, cars and Reebok trainers.

What these activists want is parity of income, regardless of effort. They think the feckless should enjoy the fruits of everyone else's labours without lifting a finger. And the more 'poor' there are to rely on benefits, the more jobs there are for the 'caring' professions.

The Tories have failed to tackle the poverty racket. In fact, in fifteen years it has got worse, especially under John Major who, when he was asked if it was the job of government to reduce inequality, unthinkingly replied: 'Yes'. No it isn't. It is the job of government to increase equality of opportunity and provide a humane safety net. Politicians shy away from the truth about 'poverty' for fear of upsetting the begging industry and the *Guardian*-reading classes. It is remarkable the way a Conservative government has swallowed a socialist agenda. But no one has satisfactorily explained to me exactly when 'a chicken in every pot' became 'a BMW in every driveway'.

SIT ON MY QUANGO AND TELL ME THAT YOU LOVE ME

I'm not quite sure when Britain ceased to be a democracy. I'm not sure it ever has been. But what is certain is that over the past fifteen years the business of government and so-called public 'service' has become even less accountable to those of us who pay for it. A third of all public spending in Britain is now controlled by unelected quangos. At the last count there were 5521 of these bodies, with budgets totalling £46.6 million. There are 73,000 quango members, all appointed. They outnumber local councillors by three to one. They control every area of our national life – doing everything from running schools, hospitals and fire brigades to framing laws and inventing 'guidelines', deciding what we watch on TV and listen to on the wireless (see chapter elsewhere on the Radio Authority) and implementing notions of political correctness. They are answerable to no one.

There is a parallel universe out there, sustained by public money, in which those of us who are paying for it play no part other than picking up the bill. Here's an example: Those of us who sometimes despair that the BBC is being suffocated by political correctness were heartened by a 'Panorama' documentary last September about teenage girls getting pregnant to jump the council housing queue and claim extra benefits. It was a splendid piece of

investigative journalism, without a bleeding heart in sight.
Until after it was broadcast, that is. Then the forces of
outrage swung into action. And the Broadcasting
Complaints Commission upheld a complaint about the
programme from the National Council for One-Parent
Families. The Council alleged that 'Babies on Benefit' was
misleading and unfair, even though there was not a single
complaint from anyone featured in it. And under the 1990
Broadcasting Act, only a person with a direct interest in a
programme can complain. Which is why the High Court
rejected the Commission's ruling, adding that if it had been
upheld it would send clear signals to BBC journalists to
'steer clear of politically incorrect' themes.

The National Council for One-Parent Families is a classic
example of an organisation which takes offence on behalf of
others for a living and wants to censor that which it finds
politically inconvenient. It claims to represent 1.3 million
people and receives £650,000 a year from government. But
it has fewer than 5000 members, most of them from public
corporations, other pressure groups and local authorities.
There is no evidence of single parents queuing up to join in
their hundreds of thousands. It has a vested interest in
complaining about programmes like 'Babies on Benefit'.
Just as the assorted race relations and equal opportunities
quangos have a vested interest in seeking out inequality and
discrimination where none exists. Organisations like this
take offence where there is none remotely taken by those
directly involved, in order to justify their own irrelevant
and expensive existence.

So we end up with a State-funded broadcaster and two
State-funded quangos involved in a costly court case paid
for by the taxpayer. It doesn't end here, either. The
Commission was given leave to appeal. The appeal was
ending when I finished this book. Goodness knows how

much all this cost us. My one hope is that 'Panorama' will, at the end of it all, look into the money spent by the National Council for One-Parent Families and the Broadcasting Complaints Commission.

SIT ON MY CHANGO AND TELL ME THAT YOU LOVE ME 168

much all this cost us. My one hope is that Panorama will,
at the end of it all, look into the money spent by the
National Council for One-Parent Families and the broadcasting

PRIME MINISTER'S QUESTION TIME DOWN THE DOG AND DUCK

Nothing better illustrates the lack of democracy and
accountability in Britain than the fiasco called Prime
Minister's Question Time. This is supposed to be the
occasion, twice a week, for fifteen minutes, when the Prime
Minister has to face questions from back-bench MPs and is
called to account for his actions in front of the House and the
whole nation, watching on television. It is an opportunity
for ordinary members to bring the concerns of their
constituents to the Prime Minister's attention. That's why
so many questions go something like: 'Is the Prime Minister
aware that the good people of Melchester are deeply
unhappy about the price of gobstoppers?' If an MP from the
government benches is asking the question, the PM will
agree that he, too, is as concerned as the Honourable
Gentleman's constituents about the price of gobstoppers
and has asked the Minister of Gobstoppers to look into it
immediately. If it is an Opposition MP, the PM will reply
angrily – raising his voice and banging the dispatch box –
that during the period of the last Labour government – as a
direct result of rampant socialism and trades union bullying
and the dead not getting buried – the price of gobstoppers
rose by at least twelve times the rate of inflation. Furthermore, thanks to thirteen years of Tory government, our
gobstopper prices are now the envy of the Universe.

All this is a complete waste of time – a glorified wank. Five minutes of valuable parliamentary time has been used up. The Prime Minister has avoided being put on the spot over something which really matters and no one has emerged any the wiser. The one beneficiary is the MP for Melchester, who has managed to get his ugly mug on the telly and say 'Melchester' a couple of times. Mind you, I'm not convinced that it does the MP much good with his constituents. Most of these MPs come across as complete tossers.

The worst kind is the member who gets to his hind legs and asks the Prime Minister: 'Would the Prime Minister agree that the Opposition is comprised entirely of child molesters, communists and terrorists, who would take this country into a federal union with Red China and Nicaragua, put taxes up to 150p in the pound, make homosexuality compulsory in schools and order the slaughter of the first-born?' What the hell is the PM supposed to reply? 'I thank the honourable member for his question but I must say he does seem to have lost complete control of his senses. I can only assume he has been in Annie's Bar since it opened. My honourable friends on the Opposition benches might be a bit fond of the unions and putting a few pence on the top rate of income tax but over and above that the honourable member is talking complete bollocks in an attempt to ingratiate himself with his constituency party and get himself on the honours list.'

That's what he should say. Of course, he won't. He knows the game. This is what he will reply: 'I thank the honourable member for his question and bringing the dangers inherent in a Labour government to the attention of the House and the whole nation. Under the last Labour administration, people may have forgotten, the country was run by child molesters and IRA terrorists, income tax was actually £5 in the £ and the schools were run by drug dealers and lesbians.' Everyone with half a brain knows this is a complete and utter waste of time and does as much as anything else – probably more – to bring the whole political process into disrepute. Yet there is still no shortage of MPs willing to jump up and down like jack-in-the-boxes and shout their heads off during Prime Minister's Question Time.

One who jumps higher and yells louder than most is David Amess, the publicity-seeking Tory MP for Basildon whose success in holding the key Essex marginal signalled the Tories' unexpected general election victory in 1992 and who is likely to be the first casualty whenever Major decides to tie the rope round his neck, jump off the chair and call the next election. Amess featured in an exchange in this parliament which, more than any other, illustrates exactly what is wrong with Prime Minister's Question Time. What the people of Basildon want to know is why, after helping to return a Conservative government, so many of them have lost their homes, lost their jobs, lost their businesses and are paying more tax than they were under Labour in the 1970s? They might actually have wanted their MP to ask why the PM was hell-bent on dragging Britain into a federal Europe. Amess might have asked if John Major was aware that unemployment in Basildon had increased by nearly 200 per cent since he became Prime Minister. He might have asked if the PM was aware that the Army and Navy stores and dozens of other smaller shops in Basildon had closed as a direct result of Conservative economic policy.

But when Amess's big moment came, this is what Hansard records that he actually said: 'Is the Prime Minister aware that mortgage interest rates for first-time buyers are now at their lowest level for twenty-five years? Does he agree that that will have the effect of putting more money in people's pockets so that they can spend it on goods in the High Street and thereby help our economic recovery? Does he further agree that this is very good news for home buyers throughout Basildon?'

Funnily enough, the Prime Minister did agree. He was hardly going to do otherwise. God knows what the disaffected, disillusioned voters of Basildon made of it. None of this struck me as the burning issue to the Dog and Duck, Basildon.

'Oi, Jason, did you know that mortgage rates for first-time buyers are now at their lowest level for twenty-five years?'

'That is good news, Tel. It should have the effect of putting more money into people's pockets so that they can spend it on goods in the High Street and thereby help our economic recovery.'

'You are not wrong, Jase, my old son. You'd have to agree that this is very good news for home buyers throughout Basildon.'

'Not many, Tel. Another lager top?'

'Why not? Now that mortgage rates for first-time buyers are at their lowest level for twenty-five years we've all got more money in our pockets. I might pop down the High Street later and help the economic recovery.'

'Cheers, Tel. Here's to the Tories.'

Precisely.

Either Question Time reverts to its original purpose of making the Prime Minister accountable or it should be scrapped all together. What we get twice a week is a cynical, patronising party political broadcast, all wind and piss. Tony Blair is said privately to be deeply unhappy about Question Time. In which case he should refuse to take part, on the grounds that it is a complete sham. Most people are sick and tired of parliamentary posturing. The politician who realises that and has the courage to do something about it will have earned our eternal gratitude.

RADIO DAZE

After twenty years in the print, a radio career beckoned. My broadcasting experience had been limited to a few appearances as a performing seal on pundit panels on other people's programmes, when, in the summer of 1991, I was asked if I fancied sitting in for the regular presenter of the afternoon phone-in on London's LBC Radio. I always reckoned I had a face for radio, so what the hell. I didn't have to give up the day job. So at 1pm one sweltering Monday, a time when all sensible journalists are embarking on a serious lunch, I found myself sitting in a studio in darkest Hammersmith wondering what on earth I was going to do for the next three hours, especially if no one rang up. I was bloody terrified. What do I do now, boss? Fortunately I got away with it. The gig lasted a fortnight, after which I had to be taken away in a bucket, a quivering mess of understains and exhaustion. I was like one of those women in the Sure advert. At the end of each three-hour stint, I was wringing wet, with a giant tick on my back. I had to lie in a bath of draught Guinness for several hours before I began to feel human again. But I'd caught the bug. From then on I decided that what I wanted was my own radio show. The audience apparently liked what they heard and as a result I became LBC's dynamic Number 12 shirt, sitting in for absent presenters. The main chance came when I took over the Michael Parkinson show for two weeks at Christmas. I'd been a regular guest on Parky's Friday morning panel of news reviewers. That was a big enough deal for a hack of my generation who had grown up in awe of Parkinson, the man who defined the chat show art in this country. To be occupying the great man's chair was a singular honour. My mum was impressed.

After several stints as Parky's locum, the following summer I was given my own show. It's one thing sitting in for other presenters, but you are naturally constrained. The trick is to be competent, but not brilliant. They want a safe pair of hands, but it's bad form to take too many catches. Your job is to keep the audience happy, but make sure the star is welcomed back with open arms. You don't really get to develop your own act until you get your own circus. I've always figured that there's no point in trying to ape anyone else. It's futile me trying to write like Keith Waterhouse or Bernard Levin, they've already done it better. Similarly, if people want to listen to Michael Parkinson they might as well listen to the genuine article.

If I'd had one serious complaint about radio in Britain it was that it was too *safe*. The Reithian tradition demands balance and deference. Balance, in broadcast terms, means allowing one politician to tell lies uninterrupted, followed by an opposing politician telling a different pack of lies and then thanking them both politely. Stuff that for a game of soldiers. I was determined this show would be different. There's only so much you can do with a phone-in format, but one thing you can do is treat the callers with respect. They're the paying public. It takes great courage to call a radio show. Unless the callers are rabid nutters or paid-up, knuckle-scraping members of the BNP or the Socialist Workers' Party, then I've always tried to treat them courteously. There have been other presenters who made a

name for themselves by bullying stammering and in-
articulate first-time callers. That's like kicking cripples. It's
downright cowardly and embarrassing to listen to. It's been
my experience that such presenters can usually be found
half-way up the arses of politicians and celebrity guests. My
view was always that you treat the audience politely and the
politicians with the respect they deserve, usually none at all.

We needed a theme tune which would be a declaration of
intent. Eventually I settled on the fairground-inspired
'House of Fun' by Madness. No one was going to confuse
this show with 'Call Nick Ross'. It was my intention from
day one to blur the heavily defined line between news and
comment. 'Littlejohn's Long Lunch' – seriously – went on
the air in August 1992, in the middle of a period of crisis in
the London Ambulance Service. An expensive new
computer system had been installed to replace the 999
operators. Predictably it was complete disaster and the
radio station was inundated with callers complaining about
long delays, which some claimed had resulted in deaths. We
had an issue. For several weeks we battered away at the
story until eventually the head of the Ambulance Service
agreed to be interviewed on the phone. During the course
of our argument – I wouldn't call it a debate, it was more
like a shouting match – I told him in no uncertain terms that
he should resign. Not, *would* he resign? Or, some people
might think that perhaps he might like to consider resign-
ing, if that's all right with you, sir, gawd bless yer, you're a
toff and no mistake. At this point – it was about half past one
– he announced that he had to go. What could possibly be
more important than explaining to the people of London why
he had wrecked their ambulance service? I asked. He ummed
and ahhed and mumbled something about a meeting. I knew
then he had lost it. He was dead in the water. Within a few
days he had fallen on his sword. We were in business.

It was shortly afterwards that I became aware of something called the Radio Authority. Apparently, ever so informally at first, they had let LBC know that presenters weren't supposed to have *opinions*. Damn it all, who knows where it might end? Still, we ploughed on. Mike Lawrence, the programme controller, explained to me that we had to expand the envelope gently. I wasn't so much expanding the envelope as putting a letter bomb inside it. The show wasn't all phone-in. But with a tiny budget, I had to call in as many favours as possible to fill three hours. The splendid Anna Raeburn agreed to come in and do an agony half-hour once a week for next to nothing. In return I agreed she could tackle any subject she liked. I'll admit I aways had my doubts about whether anal sex was a suitable early-afternoon topic. But my producer assured me it was the sort of thing 'Woman's Hour' would tackle and was therefore perfectly proper. In retrospect, it was a mistake to take calls. It was asking for trouble. Maybe I shouldn't have started laughing when Anna described the 'flora and fauna' to be found up the average back passage. Still, no harm done, I thought. I thought wrong. Three weeks after the show went on air, I heard officially from the Radio Authority. This was not a way to behave at 2.30pm in the afternoon. I had been warned. LBC veterans said they had heard nothing like it since a woman had rung up one evening and described, on air, how much she enjoyed oral sex with her Alsatian. She particularly liked his rough tongue, a few thousand listeners heard her say before the plug was pulled. The tape is still changing hands for serious money.

With no budget to speak of, I took to bribing my Fleet Street friends to come on the programme by promising them strong drink. Every Friday, I would fill the studio with champagne and invite a few of the lads along. Nigel Dempster, the *Daily Mail* diarist, arrived in expansive, post-prandial mood and declared that he had regularly been buggered at school and it had never done him any harm. As he spoke, I swore I saw the ghost of Anna Raeburn wander across the studio. Charlie Catchpole, the *News of the World* TV critic, was discussing the late, unlamented North Sea soap opera 'Triangle' when I happened to suggest that if they'd have called it 'Kate O'Mara's Triangle' – in the spirit of 'Bob's Full House' – they might have got a bigger audience. The studio guests collapsed in a fit of giggles and one listener phoned in to say he had mounted the kerb in his car and hit a waste-paper bin. The following week, LBC received a warning from the Radio Authority after someone complained that we were drunk on air. An outrageous suggestion. (Catchpole was also involved in a much-later on-air boozing session during my morning show, when the *Reservoir Dogs* director Quentin Tarantino helped our three regular arts critics and me demolish seven bottles of Beaujolais Nouveau between 11am and midday. Quentin obviously enjoyed himself. When he returned to England a couple of months later, he rang and asked if he could come back. He obviously thought we always drank that much on a Thursday morning. Not at all. Sometimes we drank even more.)

'Littlejohn's Long Lunch' was a mercifully short-lived affair. In September, Michael Parkinson announced that he was giving up his popular morning show to spend more time with his golf clubs. Parky described the five-mornings-a-week, three-hour show as living in a state of permanent jet lag – something I was about to discover. Whatever shambles 'Littlejohn's Long Lunch' seemed to those involved, it was a ratings success. So as Parky headed for the first tee, it was Richard Littlejohn, Come On Down. 'Littlejohn's Long Lunch' lived on in spirit, if not in name. The tone of the morning show was sceptical and irreverent. It was wireless with attitude.

The first hour was still given over to phone-in. We kicked off in the wake of Black Wednesday and the programme became a focus for public disenchantment with the Tories. Sitting on the fence just gets you splinters in your arse. In my opening editorials I went for the jugular – campaigning for a referendum on Maastricht and the resignation of a number of ministers, including John Major. All, it must be said, spectacularly unsuccessfully. Well, not all. I can recall the disgraced minister David Mellor – who resigned from the Cabinet over his affair with an actress and his free holidays paid for by the daughter of a leading PLO official – accusing me of indulging in 'populist tub-thumping'. He added: 'That will get you nowhere.' To which I replied: 'It got rid of you.' One-nil.

I knew we had hit a raw nerve. All the pent-up anger that Londoners felt with Major's government spewed out on the air. We were turning callers away at the end of the first hour every day. It might sound pompous, but I believe this was democracy in action – about the only chance taxpayers get to vent their feelings other than at election time. I had no intention of complying with the Radio Authority's idea of 'balance'. If politicians were lying, I said so. I knew from executives at LBC that the Establishment was getting uncomfortable with our daily diatribe against politicians and political correctness. But the ratings were soaring, so they gave me my head. It was after one of our frequent debates on the future of the royal family that I heard again from the Radio Authority. I had raised a few eyebrows on an earlier show when I remarked that I would lose no sleep if there was a member of the royal family dangling from every lamp-post in The Mall. This time, as *Daily Express* diarist Ross Benson was citing the royals as a shining example to the nation, I happened to ask: 'What kind of example is a tax-evading bunch of adulterers?' The klaxons went off in the Radio Authority's bunker. Someone complained. Suddenly their gongs were in danger. LBC received another official broadside.

I never officially discovered who complained – they never tell you. But I was unofficially informed that it was a well-known left-wing Labour MP, no friend of the royals, who was settling an old score. Malicious, the complaint may have been. Nonsensical, the bollocking certainly was. But because of the way radio franchises are awarded in this country, LBC – whose licence was due for renewal – began to twitch and asked me to cool it. I agreed – and then totally ignored what they said. (Either the Radio Authority gave up or they failed to hear me describing the Princess of Wales and the Duchess of York as a 'pair of old slappers'. Whatever, I got away with that one.)

At the time I was running back-to-back with the robust, quick-witted and equally anti-Establishment Australian Mike Carlton, who presented the breakfast show. Carlton was the man once suspended for announcing 'I'm pissed as a parrot' at 6.00am. Every morning, the great and the good would be treated to six hours of abuse on London's commercial talk station. While politicians were being addressed on Radio 4 'with the greatest of possible respect', on 97.3FM the Prime Minister was being described as a 'hopeless berk'. At the height of the Maastricht débâcle, I called on air for him to be prosecuted for high treason.

Whether Carlton and I influenced the Radio Authority's decision to strip LBC of both its licences – and replace it with a nice, safe rolling news format – is open to speculation. Lord Chalfont, the Establishment placeman who ran the authority, always refused to give proper reasons and declined to come on to my programme and explain to the people of London why he was taking LBC off the air. Chalfont – a defence hack turned Tory fund-raiser – did tell the BBC that he thought some presenters – no names, no pack drill – too freely mixed fact and comment and complained that there were too many phone-ins. Politicians hate phone-ins. They think the electorate should only express an opinion once every five years, and then in silence, in private, in a secret ballot with an ever-diminishing choice of policies. Of course, no one ever voted for Chalfont, or anyone else on the Radio Authority. He was apparently not accountable to anyone. Listeners who wrote to Number 10 protesting about the decision received a reply which said the Radio Authority was nothing to do with the Prime Minister, the government or the Conservative Party. MPs who took up the cudgels discovered it was not accountable to parliament, either. So who the hell does it answer to? The Radio Authority is one of the unelected quangos which take so many decisions which affect our lives these days. Elsewhere in the book, I devote a whole chapter to quangos, which have multiplied exponentially in the last decade. So much for democracy. So much for free speech.

Once the death sentence on LBC had been passed, there was a stay of execution of twelve months. I determined to use my remaining time on the air to embarrass the authority as often as possible and expose its members to the cold light of publicity. I started by reading out the names of every single one of them, their CVs, their family histories, their occupations. They were the usual procession of politically-correct, ethnically-balanced non-entities who are appointed to such committees. They had sat in judgement on LBC, even though most of them lived outside London and rarely heard the station. They ignored the wishes of the people of London and the audience figures, which were steadily increasing. The ratings for my own show had gone up by 60 per cent in a year.

I continued to ridicule Chalfont at every available opportunity until I ran out of road and decided to leave LBC in February 1994, not only because the station was going nowhere but because I had begun to suffer seriously from Parky's jet lag. I didn't realise just how knackered I was until I stopped. It was a difficult decision. I loved the daily touchstone with the people of London. No matter how dreadful or hungover I felt at 9.00am, once Madness had blown away the cobwebs, I'd got my monologue out of my system and had opened the phone lines I was back on the case. John Major wanked on about being at the heart of Europe. He should find out what it feels like to be at the heart of London. When I walked out of LBC for the last time and into the Albion over the road, I thought I'd heard the last of the Radio Authority. Not so.

A couple of months after I left I received two posthumous bollockings from Chalfont's cavaliers. The first arose from an interview with the celebrated feminist writer and activist Erin Pizzey, who complained that the women's movement had been taken over by men-hating 'fascists'. I agreed with her, adding that what seems to have happened to feminism is what has happened to most good causes – it has been hijacked by nutters, in this case 'hatchet-faced, shaven-headed dykes in boiler suits who despise men'. One listener – again, I wasn't allowed to know whom – complained about the term 'hatchet-faced dyke', which I had used on the wireless before, most notably when referring to the hatchet-faced dyke headmistress who banned her children from watching *Romeo and Juliet*, discussed elsewhere. The forces of regulation and censorship stirred into action and, after the usual round of lunches and expenses, decided I had contravened the Broadcasting Act 1990 Section 90(1)(a) and the Radio Authority Programme Code Rule 1.2 Sex. LBC was reprimanded, even though I had long since left. The second, more serious, complaint concerned remarks I had made the morning after a violent demonstration outside the House of Commons as MPs voted on lowering the homosexual age of consent. The authority helpfully provided a transcript of my opening monologue:

> . . . Our MPs on parade today are Charles Kennedy, Diane Abbott and Peter Bottomley, and I'll be asking them, amongst other things, why they voted to allow schoolboys to be buggered at sixteen.
>
> Curious woman, Edwina Currie. A couple of years ago she wanted to ban all eggs on the grounds that they're a threat to health. Now she demands legalised teenage anal sex – the surest and quickest way of transmitting AIDS.
>
> Call me old-fashioned, but I'd rather have a runny omelette. As I said yesterday, the age of consent isn't anything I lose sleep worrying about and I couldn't care less where it is, although I think the decision to peg it at eighteen was about right.
>
> However, seeing the plankton bouncing up and down outside the Commons last night, if I were an MP I'd have probably voted to raise the age to sixty-five and banned moustaches and earrings as a basis for negotiation.
>
> Anything which that lot outside the Commons are in favour of, I'm against in principle. The police should have turned the dogs on 'em – and if that failed brought out the flamethrowers . . .

About par for the course. Nothing regular listeners were not familiar with. My newspaper column the following day made similar points. I didn't receive a single letter of complaint. But someone did complain to the Radio Authority, alleging that 'the degree of bigotry beggared belief' – perhaps that should be buggered belief – and labelling me not only a homophobe by claiming my 'general demeanour was reminiscent of Nazi Germany'. Where do they find these people? Can't they differentiate between starting a world war and sending millions to the gas chamber and objecting to a copper being kicked unconscious by a bunch of militant homosexuals over the issue of whether or not schoolboys can legally take it up the arse? Obviously not. After more lunches and expenses, the authority threw the book at me.

This time I had not only breached the Broadcasting Act Section 90(1)(a) and Radio Authority Programme Code Rule 1.2 Sex but also Radio Authority Programme Code Rule 1.5 Portrayal of Violence. It was decreed that I was a homophobe and had incited violence. This was despite the fact that LBC wrote to the authority pointing out that both my programme editor and studio engineer were gay and saw nothing offensive in my 'general demeanour'. In fact, they thought it was hilarious. None of the homosexuals employed at LBC voiced any objection – and there were enough of them. As I remarked on air: 'You can't swing a handbag in this place without hitting at least half a dozen.' LBC also pointed out that I had taken a large number of calls both for and against the demonstration, including a couple who moved on to discuss the merits of Torville and Dean before bidding me a fond farewell. No one who listened to the programme could have believed for a moment that I was inciting violence. Instead the authority chose to side with a bunch of thugs who had beaten up a police officer.

In both of these cases I was found guilty in my absence, without actually knowing I was being tried and without being told the name of my accuser. What was that about Nazi Germany? The authority decided that this was such a serious offence that it warranted a severe financial penalty – in theory LBC could have been fined tens of thousands of pounds. But the fine was waived because LBC was in receivership. And why was it in receivership? Er, because the Radio Authority had taken its licence away.

These daft rules exist to give people like Lord Chalfont – now, thankfully, departed from the Radio Authority – something to do, not to protect the public. The Public Order Act is already sufficient to prevent incitement to violence. No case against me would have stood up in a court of law. On the evening I received news of my reprimand I happened across a Channel Four programme about lesbians, featuring a shaven-headed lesbian comedienne (-ian?) shouting at the top of her voice: 'I'm a big dyke!' You couldn't get on the radio with stuff like that.

Still, complaints are an occupational hazard of my job. I suppose they prove you're doing your job properly. The world is full of sad nobodies scouring the newspapers and airwaves for something to complain about. More often than not they are lonely, premature ejaculators in anoraks and ugly, frustrated spinsters with nothing better to do of an evening and no hope of getting a proper job or someone to share their empty lives – let alone their soiled nylon duvets, encrusted with muesli droppings and stray bits of Cadbury's Flake. Either that or they are professional busybodies on thirty grand a year and a Citroën diesel estate, with a Nuclear Power No Thanks sticker in the back window, taking offence on behalf of someone else. Sometimes they are to be found in the dark, smelly corners of those health food restaurants where outreach co-ordinators gather to gorge themselves on high-fibre food – which tastes like shredded cardboard and with any luck will rip their insides out – while they plan the revolution and whinge about lack of 'resources' for traffic humps and Eritrean lesbians. (There's one of these health food restaurants near where I live. The one thing the customers all have in common – apart from clothes which have never seen the inside of an Indesit and hair which appears to have been washed in stagnant sump oil – is that they all look ill.) Most of the time they sit festering in dank bedsits, drinking Belgian red wine, practising solitary vices and shouting at 'Newsnight' on old black and white portable televisions with useless indoor aerials. Part of the fun is winding them up. If it keeps them off the streets, so much the better. The best thing to do is ignore them and hope that one day they will be found dangling from a rafter in their attic, wearing nothing but a frogman's helmet and a faded Free Nelson Mandela T-shirt, with a satsuma between their teeth and a rolled-up copy of the *Guardian* jobs supplement clenched between their buttocks. It is my mission in life to make these people as miserable as possible. It seems to be working. The golden rule is never to write back to these nutters. It only encourages them. Eventually they get bored and turn their attention to something else, like chaining themselves to trees in the path of motorway extensions or nipple piercing.

When I left LBC Radio and headed off to Sky and London Weekend Television, I entered a new world of regulation. After news of my new TV career in the papers, I was sent a copy of the LWT duty officer's report for Friday 6 May 1994, which logs all calls from viewers for the Independent Television Commission. It contained routine grumbles about popular shows such as 'Play Your Cards Right', 'Surprise Surprise' and 'Gladiators'. It also contained the following entry, timed at 19.38 hours: '*Viewer has heard there is to be a programme with Richard Littlejohn and advises us to drop it before it goes any further.*' The show wasn't due to start for another two months. It's the first time I've ever received a complaint in advance!

WHERE'S FRIAR TUCK, THEN?

The Americans pioneered the concept of the rainbow coalition, Ken Livingstone and the old Labour GLC imported it to Britain. It works on the theory that everyone – or just about everyone – is a victim, a member of a minority. And if you then single each 'minority' for special treatment, after convincing them they are being discriminated against and need to be compensated, they will be eternally grateful and return you to office in perpetuity. Well, that's the theory anyway.

In America you don't actually meet any Americans any more. They're all Irish-Americans, or Italian-Americans, or African-Americans, even if they've never been anywhere near Ireland, Italy or Africa in their lives or couldn't point to them on a map. The Red Indians are in on the act, too, answering to the name of Native Americans. It is becoming fashionable over here now. That's because there's money to be made by proving you're a minority and are being victimised. I'm beginning to realise where I've been going wrong for all these years. If I had a pound for every time I've been asked 'Where's Friar Tuck, then?' I'd be a rich man. Instead of laughing it off I should have filed a complaint to an industrial tribunal. Then maybe I really would be, if not a rich man, at least a few grand better off. I'm not sure I qualify for assistance from the Commission for Racial

Equality, but it can only be a matter of time. As a white Essex male I am a member of the most abused and prosecuted minority in Britain. (We're about the only group in Haringey without our own outreach department and cultural centre. I must have a word with Bernie Grant to see if he can be persuaded to take up our cause. Perhaps if we throw a few petrol bombs and kill a copper he might do something for us. That usually does the trick.) Even though I am probably qualified to play football for Ireland, on account of a long and meaningful relationship with draught Guinness, I doubt I would receive much sympathy from the humour police at the CRE.

Unlike machinist Trevor McAuley, who was awarded £6000 compensation after complaining that he was the butt of Irish jokes at work. A tribunal ruled in his favour, even though there was absolutely no evidence to support his allegations and his union had advised him against pursuing his claim. But the prosection in cases involving political correctness – rather like Senator McCarthy –requires no hard evidence. The defendant is always guilty unless he can prove his innocence. The CRE backed Mr McAuley – in other words, we paid for it – and opened the door to thousands of similar cases. 'We are looking forward to tribunals making much larger awards, maybe twice or three times as much,' said the commission's legal officer Chris Bootham.

I bet they are – especially as the ceiling on racial discrimination awards has been abolished – not by British Parliament but by directive from the unelected European Commission, which John Major says he doesn't allow to interfere with our affairs, oh no. It follows the scrapping of the limit in sex discrimination cases, which has led to the obscenity of those greedy, stupid women who broke their contract of employment with the RAF and fell pregnant –

including one silly cow who got herself up the duff by a Roman Catholic priest – being awarded compensation of thousands of pounds out of the public purse. No wonder the CRE licked its lips in anticipation. All those lovely claims, all that expensive paperwork, all those new jobs.

The ruling must have come as something of a relief to the Commission, which had been running out of trouble to make. It was set up, entirely properly, to prevent people being discriminated against on grounds of race, creed or colour – primarily blacks and Asians – in housing and unemployment. Only the sort of bigot you find throwing bottles on Anti-Nazi League marches would not concede that things have improved beyond all measure. And you might have thought that with the improving race relations climate, the CRE should be scaling down its operations. Instead it is expanding into new areas. Like every other quango, it has now got completely out of hand and taken on a life of its own, hiring at will and consuming millions of pounds every year. CRE chairman Herman Ouseley was recently reduced to asking white people to make complaints about racial discrimination to try to justify its existence. You couldn't make it up, could you?

This is absolute madness. There will be a backlash and when it comes it will be ferocious. In the United States it has already begun. American males are rebelling against thirty years of 'affirmative action' and have launched a campaign to repeal all the laws discriminating in favour of women and blacks. In a few weeks, men in California managed to collect 616,000 signatures to force a statewide referendum. A group calling itself the Civil Rights Initiative is seeking to ban all state institutions from using 'race, sex, colour, ethnicity or national origin' as a criterion for discriminating against or granting preference to any individual or group. It is estimated that scrapping all the affirmative action programmes in the state would save taxpayers £80 million a year. The initiative has some powerful backers, including the Republican presidential candidate Pat Buchanan.

Ordinary white males in America feel disenfranchised and discriminated against. There is a rich vein of discontent which has been tapped into by right-wing radio talk-show hosts such as Rush Limbaugh. White men believe they suffer widespread discrimination in offices and factories. The sponsors of the initiative say they want a colourblind society with individual rights rather than group entitlements. I wouldn't suggest that the situation in Britain is anywhere near as bad as it is in the USA, but there are worrying signs. And the kind of resentment fostered by political correctness in the workplace and in the allocation of jobs, housing and benefit can act as a persuasive recruiting sergeant for extremist groups. Intelligent commentators have already picked up on it. My LWT colleague Darcus Howe – himself West Indian – has written that blacks should be given jobs on merit and not because of the colour of their skin. Some prominent blacks like Howe believe the race relations industry is itself patronising and a bar to real progress.

If we are to avoid the kind of backlash now underway in the USA we have to scrap the CRE and abandon the kind of tribunal system which awards £6000 compensation for an Irish joke without any evidence to support it.

ROYAL FLUSH

In October 1991, following a series of articles I had written attacking the royal family, the BBC asked me to present a programme called 'Fifth Column'. I was asked to give a personal opinion why the monarchy should be abolished and the Queen forced to pay taxes. Two days before the show was due to be transmitted, the Beeb pulled the plug. I never did receive a proper explanation, other than the fact that the producer thought it 'too sarcastic' and 'too personal'. I rang the producer's boss seeking clarification, but he didn't have the manners to call me back. The full script lasts twenty minutes. Here are the edited highlights:

Support for the monarchy demands the suspension of rational judgement. The Queen, of course, does a very DIFFICULT job. None of us would want to swap places with her, or so we are told. Why not? Apart from being forced to turn up for the odd ceremonial obligation and having the Prime Minister round for coffee once a week, her duties aren't all that onerous. I could do that. Gissa job.

Constitutionally, the Queen should have been made redundant years ago. While she still has to give her consent to Acts of Parliament, it is a mere formality. Her position depends on her agreeing to everything that is put in front of her. If she refused to give the royal rubber stamp to any piece of legislation, the politicians would simply change the rules.

She wouldn't, of course, be handed her P45, because she doesn't have one. Her Majesty resolutely refuses to pay a penny in income tax despite having amassed a fortune conservatively estimated at £6.6 billion and growing. The coming session of parliament will be dominated by arguments about the amount of money allocated to education, transport, the environment and, particularly, the National Health Service. If the richest woman in the world paid taxes like the rest of us, the government would have more to spend. If she simply agreed to maintain the royal yacht Britannia, the Queen's flight and pay for the upkeep of the assorted royal residences out of her own vast wealth, there would be an extra £33.7 million a year up front to spend on cancer wards and classrooms.

The Queen's tax-exempt status is obscene, especially at a time when people are being prosecuted because they can't afford to pay their poll tax and their possessions are being seized by bailiffs acting in Her Majesty's name.

There is an important principle at stake here. How can we justify pursuing ordinary citizens for non-payment of taxes when the super-rich head of state does not herself have to contribute a brass farthing? There was a recent case of a hospital unit being closed for lack of cash, only months after being officially opened by the Queen. Even if she doesn't pay tax, couldn't she simply have written out a cheque to keep it open? A few million here or there wouldn't even dent the royal petty cash. Yet from what I can gather, there is no record of any member of the royal family ever making a sizeable donation of their own money to charity. Of course, many members of the royal family give their patronage to a wide range of charities. This is the justification for their nice little earners from the civil list. Royalists maintain that they *would give up their charitable work if the State stopped paying them. Surely that is an insult to their integrity? Is it seriously being suggested that the royals are so mean-spirited that they would abandon their good deeds if their backhanders dried up? If they want to be paid for charitable work, they can always apply for a job at Oxfam.*

I'm not denying that the Queen takes her work seriously. But there is no job for her to do. We don't need a head of state. We've got far too many layers of government as it is. Germany, France and the United States all manage quite nicely without a monarch, yet whenever anyone calls for an end to the monarchy, the knee-jerk reaction is always 'Why don't you go and live in Russia?'

To be fair to the Queen, at least she refrains from delivering hysterical lectures to the nation on how we must behave, unlike her husband and eldest son. Prince Philip's latest pearl of wisdom is a warning about the conseqeunces of over-population. That's a bit rich coming from a man who has brought more than the average number of offspring into the world and spent his life living off the state. It was almost on a par with his exhortation to British industrialists to pull their fingers out, despite never having done a proper day's work in his life. Prince Charles is always droning on about the environment and criticising our reliance on the car. But here is a man with more motors than Kennings – including an eight-miles-per-gallon Bentley, which he had one of his flunkies drive all the way to Czechoslovakia for an official visit, guzzling fossil fuels and puncturing the ozone layer all the way there. Similarly he wrings his hands over the plight of the homeless while evicting squatters from empty properties on his Duchy of Cornwall land. And I never thought anyone would make me feel sorry for architects. Whether you agree with what he says or not, Charles exercises power without responsibility. A few words from him can wreck a career.

And then there's the Princess of Wales. Isn't she lovely? She always looks a million dollars. Well, that's hardly surprising. Since she got married, she had spent £1.2 million on clothes. She's got more shoes than Imelda Marcos and reportedly thinks nothing of spending £70 on a single pair of knickers. As her husband only pays tax at the basic rate, no doubt he can afford it.

Still, she pulls in the crowds. But then so does Madonna. We are constantly being told that the royal family is a valuable tourist attraction. But the tourists come to see the buildings and the soldiers in fancy dress. When was the last time you heard of the Queen showing a coach party of Japanese tourists round Buck House? Alton Towers is a valuable tourist attraction, too. But the bloke who owns it still has to pay his taxes.

So why do we put up with this circus? I suppose, if nothing else, they help to sell newspapers. There is no question that people like reading about them. There has always been a fascination with the rich, famous and privileged. But curiosity should not be confused with endorsement. The respect and affection shown by our parents' generation has not been passed down. The Queen and her clan are an expensive anachronism. The royal family underpins the whole rotten edifice of privilege and snobbery. John Major says he wants a classless society. He could start by casting the Queen adrift from the constitution and making her pay taxes. Have a nice day tomorrow, Ma'am. Enjoy it while you can. I suppose a knighthood's out of the question?

That never got broadcast. It was obviously considered too controversial for 1991.

In light of what has happened since, it now looks to be fairly mild stuff. In 1995, it's impossible to be 'too sarcastic' and 'too personal' about the monarchy. I like to think I have played my small part in changing people's perceptions. I felt it was finally worth giving this old script an airing in this book to demonstrate just how much things have changed.

Six years ago, whenever I criticised the royal family my postbag was full of hate mail. Since then the royal family seems to have gone into self-destruct mode, culminating in the acrimonious Diana-Charles split, the Tampax tapes, the annus horribilis and the Queen agreeing to pay income tax – up to a point. The antics of the younger royals have done most to bring the game into disrepute. After years of making the constitutional case for abolition of the monarchy, some of us don't mind if it has taken personalities to persuade the public to our point of view. And if there is now a majority in favour of ending the monarchy, then we must primarily thank the Prince and Princess of Wales. Ever since their separation, they have been involved in an unseemly and increasingly desperate squabble for the public's affection. All, happily, to no avail.

Throughout I have maintained a barrage of ridicule. And there's been plenty of ammunition.

There is no gimmick Diana won't employ to try to win us over, from weeping crocodile tears in public, through shaking hands with AIDS victims, to going bra-less on holiday. I have to say, the pictures of her without her Wonderbra were far less flattering than those taken without her permission in a west London gym – over which she sued the *Daily Mirror*. Am I the only man on earth who finds Lady Di completely sexless, no matter how hard she tries to be alluring? She's always reminded me of one of those shop window mannequins – looks fine from a distance, but when you get up close you discover there are no naughty bits.

When Diana split from Charles, she announced that she wanted to remain an 'independent' member of the royal family. I remember remarking at the time that it was a bit like Bianca Jagger announcing that she wished to remain an independent member of the Rolling Stones. The Windsors are like the Corleone family. Blood is thicker than marriage. She was always going to get frozen out. And so it has proved. Perhaps the final straw was when Charles went on nationwide television with Jonathan Dimbleby and admitted his long-time affair with Camilla Parker-Bowles – ending all speculation about a reconciliation for the sake of the monarchy and the sake of the children.

The Dimbleby interview was instructive, but I couldn't help feeling that there was something missing. So I scoured the cutting room floor for out-takes. This is what I found:

DIMBLEBY: Let's talk about the state of your relationship with the Princess of Wales.

CHARLES: Must we discuss that scheming little bitch?

DIMBLEBY: I'm afraid so.

CHARLES: Well, David, I've never liked her, you know. Only married her for the son and heir and one for luck.

DIMBLEBY: There has been talk of a reconciliation.

CHARLES: Not bloody likely. The sooner I get shot of her altogether, the better. Look at this Barclaycard bill. She cost me 160 grand last year.

DIMBLEBY: Surely you don't begrudge her some luxuries?

CHARLES: There are limits, for heaven's sake. Colonic irrigation, £5000. Five bloody grand. She could have come out to Highgrove and I'd have hooked her up to the hosepipe in the stables. Wouldn't have cost a penny.

DIMBLEBY: What about her clothes bill?

CHARLES: Why does she need so many frocks? Anne's still wearing the clothes she's had for twenty years. In fact, some of them used to belong to Auntie Margaret until she started hitting the sauce in a big way and grew out of them. Diana won't wear the same pair of knickers twice. I didn't used to mind, but then I discovered I was having to fork out to dress her fancy men, too. That's what I call taking the royal wee.

DIMBLEBY: I think you're being a little harsh, sir. After all, you had – how shall I put it? – a bit on the side yourself.

CHARLES: Camilla, you mean? Very game girl. Plenty of behind the settee and isn't after one's money. At least she's got some conversation. Doesn't spend all day walking round with one of those infernal bloody Sony wotsits glued to her head. Is it any wonder I ended up talking to plants?

DIMBLEBY: Let's move on to your official duties, sir. This year you celebrate twenty-five years as Prince of Wales.

CHARLES: Don't remind me, Richard. I can't stand the bloody Welsh. Maudlin race, always moaning. Totally untrustworthy. And they all think they can sing. I've lost count of the number of times I've had to stand on a hillside listening to a bunch of half-wits in blazers belting out *Men of Harlech*. Makes the heart sink, just thinking about it.

DIMBLEBY: You're well known for your concern for the environment.

CHARLES: Yes, I've always found trees and things pretty agreeable. One does what one can for the ozone layer. Did you know that emissions caused by burning fossil fuels are the biggest single threat to the planet? People should use their cars less.

DIMBLEBY: But you drive a Bentley, which only does seven miles to the gallon.

CHARLES: I'm a bloody prince, I'm entitled. I'm not talking about people like me. I'm talking about ordinary people.

DIMBLEBY: Can we turn now to the fire at Windsor Castle? That must have been terribly upsetting for you.

CHARLES: Not particularly. I'd have let it burn to the ground. It's an ugly old pile. Costs a fortune to heat it. They should have bulldozed it and put up something in concrete, more in keeping with the Slough area.

DIMBLEBY: But I thought you hated modern architecture?

CHARLES: Not at all. I love concrete – and plastic buildings. There's a marvellous new DIY warehouse on the Chipping Sodbury by-pass. It looks as if it's made of Lego. Absolutely splendid.

DIMBLEBY: But aren't you always going on about modern carbuncles?

CHARLES: You don't want to believe all that nonsense, Sir Robin. I only said it to shift a few books.

DIMBLEBY: Can we talk about your concern for wildlife?

CHARLES: Absolutely. Very keen on animals, birds, that sort of thing.

DIMBLEBY: How does that tie in with your support for hunting and fishing?

CHARLES: Damn it all, a chap's got to have a hobby. Anyway, they're my birds and animals. I can do what I like with them. It's not as if I'm shooting other people's pets.

DIMBLEBY: How will you change things when you eventually become King?

CHARLES: I might take a leaf out of King Henry VIII's book and bring back beheading for errant wives. It's much neater than divorce and a damned sight cheaper.

DIMBLEBY: It was Henry VIII who founded the Church of England. We now live in a multi-racial society. Do you think it is appropriate for a monarch to be the defender of the faith?

CHARLES: I think I should be defender of all faiths – Protestant, Catholic, Muslim, Zoroastrian.

DIMBLEBY: What's a Zoroastrian?

CHARLES: You know, those chappies with the dreadlocks and woolly hats and interesting herbal cigarettes. No Woman, No Cry.

DIMBLEBY: They're Rastafarians.

CHARLES: Same difference.

DIMBLEBY: Finally, sir, I'd like to ask what you'd have liked to have been if you hadn't been born a prince.

CHARLES: I'd like to have been a Tampax.

DIMBLEBY: CUT! Shall we try again after lunch, sir?

After the Dimbleby interview was broadcast, it was
rumoured that Diana was planning a counterstrike. She was
reported to be in discussions about granting interviews to
everyone from Oprah Winfrey and Chris Evans to Sir
David Frost.

When it was revealed that Lady Di had been having secret
talks with the legendary seventy-four-year-old American
broadcaster, Walter Cronkite, at the exclusive American
holiday resort of Martha's Vineyard to put her side of the
royal marriage saga, my imagination went into overdrive:

CRONKITE: Tonight my very special guest is the Princess of
Wales, England. Good evening, your majesty.

DI: Hello, Mr Solvite. Or, as you say in the good old US of A,
gimme five.

CRONKITE: You're very welcome, your supreme highness.

DI: Before we begin, I'd like to thank Martha for making her
home available to us.

CRONKITE: Why have you agreed to grant me this interview?

DI: Well, Walt, it is because I am so furious at old Jug Ears
hogging the headlines lately.

CRONKITE: Old Jug Ears?

DI: Yes, my husband. I'm the only one allowed to cry on the
television.

CRONKITE: I don't recall him actually crying in his interview
with Mr Michelmore.

DI: As good as, Walt. I'm sick of his self-pity. He started it,
you know. I tried, believe me I tried. But no sooner had I
changed out of my going-away outfit than he was off out the
back door like a shot to that horse-faced bint of his.

CRONKITE: Vanilla Parker-Bowles, you mean?

DI: Absolument, yah. God knows what he sees in her. Am I not the most fantastic woman on the planet? Would you climb over me to get to her?

CRONKITE: It's a long time since I climbed over anything, your royal holiness.

DI: Is that Mel Gibson over there? He's really dishy.

CRONKITE: If I may be permitted the intrusion, your royal loveliness, you have flirted with other men yourself.

DI: Hewitt, you mean? What an absolute rotter he turned out to be. Fancy flogging our story to the *Daily Express*. No one, but no one, reads the *Daily Express* any more. He should have sold it to the *Sun*.

CRONKITE: So you didn't object to it being published?

DI: Far from it. I hadn't been in the papers for a couple of days. They had to resort to using pictures of Charles.

CRONKITE: I thought you were a very private person.

DI: Oh, I am, Mr Kryptonite. And the more people who know it the better, which is why I'm talking to you tonight.

CRONKITE: You recently took action against a newspaper which published some photos of you in the gym. Why did you do that?

DI: I hadn't had time to get my eye-shadow right.

CRONKITE: May I be permitted to ask you about your private phone calls, your squidgyness?

DI: Ask all you like, Walt. They proved what a private person I really am.

CRONKITE: But do you think it is right and proper for the future Queen of England to be making small talk with a man other than her husband? What was his name, James Smirnoff?

DI: Something like that. Look, Wally, girls just wanna have fun. And if the old hubby is off rogering some wrinkly, then one is entitled to a bit of jollies of one's own.

CRONKITE: But aren't you concerned about the effect all this has on your sons?

DI: You should ask him that. He couldn't care less. He just uses them for photo opportunities, dressing them up in bloody silly kilts. Youngest one doesn't even look like him.

CRONKITE: What was it that finally brought your marriage to an end?

DI: He took exception to a frock I wanted to wear to a memorial service. I couldn't see what all the fuss was about. I looked gorgeous in it. Nobody objected when Liz Hurley wore the same dress to a film première.

CRONKITE: Why don't you get a divorce?

DI: The title comes in handy when booking a table at Daphne's. And, to be perfectly honest, I need the money. Being an international superstar doesn't come cheap. Have you seen the cost of colonic irrigation recently? You could irrigate the Sahara for the price of half-an-hour hooked up to a hosepipe in Knightsbridge. Still, he can afford it. Serves him bloody right.

CRONKITE: Have you given up all hope of becoming Queen?

DI: Given up? I am the Queen. Everybody knows that, silly. Have you seen *Four Weddings and a Funeral* yet? I went along thinking it was about the royal family. Mind you, I could do that Hugh Grant a favour.

CRONKITE: Why did you pull out of your interview with Oprah Winfrey?

DI: Two reasons. One: she thinks she's a bigger star than I am. And two: it only goes out on Channel 4 in England, so not enough people would have seen what a private person I am. Charles was on ITV, you know. Prime time. Straight after 'Coronation Street'. My favourite is Bet Lynch. Eh up, chuck. Jolly amusing. I do so like common people.

CRONKITE: Your most gracious majesty, it has been a privilege and a pleasure grovelling to you tonight.

DI: Thank you, Mr Burnett. By the way, how much am I being paid for this?

CRONKITE: Paid? No one said anything to me about money.

DI: Well, you can stuff that for a game of soldiers, sunshine. No dough, no show. Isn't that Kevin Costner over there? Kevin, Kevin . . . would you like my autograph?

DIRECTOR: CUT!

THE GOOD LIFE

Have you ever seen those adverts which go something like: 'Tired, irritable, depressed?' Or 'Tense, nervous, headache?' They're usually trying to sell you the latest miracle cure aspirin. A handful of Mother's Little Helper and, hey presto, you're immediately back on the case. Well, that's what you thought. If you play your cards right, and you're feeling tired, irritable and depressed, you could get yourself signed off sick for the next ten years, claiming disability benefit. There is apparently no ailment too trivial to qualify as a legitimate disability any more. Which might help explain why the number of people claiming disability benefit in Britain rose from 600,000 in 1980 to 1,600,000 in 1994. Are they seriously trying to tell us that there are a million more disabled people than there were fifteen years ago? Of course not. If there were, you wouldn't be able to move in the street for wheelchairs. Every time you got on a bus you'd be falling over someone's crutches.

With modern medicine, you might actually have expected the number of registered disabled to have fallen. There's no more polio, very little evidence of the debilitating respiratory diseases which used to plague Britain in the days of smog. How many people do you know who are genuinely disabled? I mean genuinely. Not just a bit off colour or down in the dumps. Or a martyr to their piles. I mean genuinely, physically disabled. So badly disabled, in fact, that it prevents them doing any kind of productive work whatsoever. So badly disabled that they have no alternative but to rely on the state for support? Er, there's whatsisname. But he lost a leg at Dunkirk. Still, didn't stop him running the bowls team for thirty-five years. And Uncle Arthur, of course. Broke his arm on the way home from the Rotary dinner. Never been the same since. And Thingy down the road. You know, him with the stick who's always down the bookie's. That's him. Gets in the King's Head. Well, now you come to mention it, like. No one you'd call, you know, disabled. Not properly, anyway. Sid's always having trouble with his lungs. Has to keep stopping on his way to Mr Patel to buy his *Sporting Life* and forty Embassy every day. But I wouldn't call him disabled, not how as you mean it like.

There are two possible explanations for the staggering rise in the number of disabled. One is that the government has been encouraging the unemployed to register as disabled in order to massage the jobless figures downwards. As someone who spent ten years as a labour correspondent and saw the count adjusted seasonally, backwards, sideways, to take account of the price of kiwi fruit and the nasty spell of weather we've been having, on twenty-three different occasions, that's an argument to which I would give some credence. But that doesn't explain everything. The truth of the matter is that every day new categories of disabled are being dreamt up by the bearded layabouts who infest the 'caring' professions. The more people they can persuade to be dependent upon them, the more work for them and others like them. Hello, is that the *Guardian* jobs page? Good. This is the outreach co-ordination department of the DSS here. Can you send us round another twenty-three politically correct carers, preferably Labour-voting non-smoking lesbians. You can, splendid. The cheque's in the post.

If you want to know where your hard-earned goes, I invite you to consider the case of Mr and Mrs Ken Watters and their five children. They only came to public attention after it was revealed that thanks to a computer error they had received an overpayment of £7000 from the DSS. What a result, eh? Especially as Mr and Mrs Watters owed £1800 in rent. Now you might have thought that the first thing they would do with this little windfall would have been to have paid off their arrears. Nothing like a bit of peace of mind, is there? That's what you and I might have done in similar circumstances. After, of course, checking to see that we were properly entitled to the dosh in the first place. Not Ken and Helen Watters, though. They went out and bought themselves a car at auction. As you do. Stands to reason, dunnit? I mean, they obviously want us to have it, don't they? We're entitled.

Had it not been for this computer error we would never have been introduced to Mr and Mrs Watters. And we would never have learned about their amazing lifestyle, entirely financed by the rest of us. Too much attention is focused on overseas nationals flooding into Britain, either legally or illegally, and living off our elaborate welfare system. The truth of the matter is that we have more than enough home-grown scroungers of our own. The Watters are the head of a festering boil of undeserving welfare beneficiaries who think the state owes them a comfortable living. And they are encouraged in this belief by the otherwise unemployable functionaries of the DSS. And when you consider what is on offer, it is hard to blame them. It all adds up as follows:

Mr Watters has not worked for ten years. He is a former forklift truck driver, who says he suffers from anxiety and agoraphobia. As a result he is payed £520 a month invalidity allowance. Since when has being anxious been a disability worthy of £520 tax-free from the state? We all get anxious from time to time. Some of us even get panic attacks. Stage fright, actors call it. We just have to suppress it and get on with our lives. I remember the first time I had to present a TV show. I was scared stiff. I felt like running away. But I didn't. I tightened my sphincter and plunged into the unknown. Not for a moment did I consider calling my GP and asking him to put me on the disabled register. Anyone who says he doesn't get anxious is a liar. Imagine how inner-city comprehensive teachers feel when they have to face another day in front of sixteen-year-old plankton with Stanley knives in their pockets. If we were all signed off sick every time we got anxious there wouldn't be a man or woman at work anywhere in the country. And agoraphobia? Couldn't they get him a job indoors?

In addition to his £520 invalidity allowance, Mr Watters also receives £170 invalidity living allowance, to help him cope with the cost of being disabled. Presumably that pays for a remote control for the video. Wouldn't want him worrying about how to programme it to record 'Neighbours', would we? The couple also receive an additional £280 housing benefit. That should stop him getting anxious about how he's going to pay the rent.

Mrs Watters has not worked for eighteen years. Apparently she's got arthritis in one leg. For that she receives her own disability allowance of £127 a month. I wonder how these things are calculated. What makes anxiety and agoraphobia worth £520 a month and a gammy leg only worth £127? Still, you will be delighted to learn that Mrs Watters doesn't go short. Her gammy leg doesn't stop her looking after her poor, disabled husband. For that she gets £136 a month from the state. At this stage you, like me, must be wondering how, if she's sick enough to get a disability allowance of £127, she can also be well enough to hold down a full-time job caring for her husband? You might also ask why she should be paid for looking after her husband. Isn't that part of the love, honour and obey deal? Why should a wife be paid for looking after her husband, especially when she herself is considered sufficiently disabled to warrant a generous disability allowance? What is it she has to do for him that he can't do for himself? Remember his official disabilities are registered as anxiety and agoraphobia. So what is it he can't do, apart from go outside to bring the milk in? I can only imagine that he's so worried about open spaces that he's frightened to go down the DSS to sign on. Perhaps that's what she does for him. Thanks to the generosity of the system, she won't have to use her free bus pass any more. One of the Watterses' daughters, Dee, has a painful knee disease. They asked the DSS for money to buy her a new pair of shoes. The DSS gave them a car instead.

I promise I am not making this up. A request for new shoes was answered with an M-reg Ford Escort, complete with free mobile telephone insurance and AA membership. (The Montego they bought with the £7000 they were given in error had by then been scrapped.) The car is leased with the aid of a further £127 disability living allowance. Now you might also be asking yourself: if Mr Watters is an anxious agoraphobic and Mrs Watters has a gammy leg, who drives the car? It is probably unwise to pursue this line of questioning. By the time this book has been published I should not be in the slightest bit surprised to learn that the Watterses have been provided with the services of a full-time chauffeur. In addition to this largesse the couple also receive child allowance of £172 a month. The Watterses had Dee and her older sister Karry when Mr Watters lost his job as a forklift truck driver. Since then they have had a further three children. I suppose if you're stuck indoors all day with anxiety, agoraphobia and a gammy leg there's little else to do until 'Home and Away' comes on the telly. But ask yourself this: if you couldn't afford to support your own existing children, would you carry on breeding even though you had no prospect of ever working again? Of course you wouldn't. But you might if a generous *Guardian* reader at the DSS told you not to worry about anything, the state will provide.

And the state has provided for the Watterses and their five children. Out of the £7000 paid in error, the kids all got new mountain bikes. Oh, and Mrs Watters treated herself to a nice new fitted kitchen. They are now pestering Wolverhampton council to give them a bigger council house, rent to be paid by the taxpayer. All told, their benefits add up to a staggering £18,500 a year. That is equivalent to a before-tax salary of £25,000 a year – well above the national average wage and way ahead of firemen on an average of £17,888, ambulance workers on £16,280, junior doctors on £13,690 and postmen on £14,300.

Is it any wonder that Mrs Watterses shows no shame or regret at living so handsomely off the rest of us? This is what she told the *Daily Mail*: 'Wages are disgusting at the moment.' Why work when the state will provide?

It has to be stressed that the Watterses are doing nothing illegal. They are perfectly entitled to every single penny they receive. They didn't even realise how much they were entitled to until it was pointed out to them by helpful welfare officials. This is after fifteen years of a Conservative government elected on a ticket of individual responsibility. A welfare system which was supposed to provide a safety net for those who had temporarily fallen on hard times has now removed the necessity and the will to work from the

Watterses of this world. They are mollycoddled by officials who have a vested interest in keeping the system expanding to feather their own nests. The madness is fuelled by politicians and lobbyists screaming for ever more 'resources'. So you start out with a system designed to make sure no one goes hungry or cold and end up with a monster consuming and regurgitating billions, paying feckless families like the Watterses more than they could ever earn by holding down a regular job and chucking in a brand-new motor into the bargain. Yet no politician has the courage to tackle this sick system and those who even dare suggest modest reforms are howled down. This is where you get £50 billion annual deficits from. If you set out to write a satire on the welfare system, you couldn't invent the Watterses. You couldn't make them up.

THE MELLORPHANT MAN

David Mellor, MP for Putney, represents everything that is rotten about the modern Conservative Party. By his deceit, his arrogance, his refusal to apologise for anything and the way he has cashed in on the notoriety brought about by his free-loading and extra-marital swordplay, and abused his sacred trust as an MP to gather a massive portfolio of directorships and consultancies, he has done more than anyone else in the House of Commons to bring the game of politics into disrepute. I've never cared who the hell he sleeps with, although I have always had some sympathy with them. And to be honest I can't see what any of them see in him. He has all the charm of a train spotter with halitosis, the wit of an undertaker and the social graces of a Rottweiler with a bellyfull of Chicken Tikka Masala. At the 'What The Papers Say' annual awards ceremony he even had the cheek to thank Piers Morgan, the editor of the *News of the World*, for exposing his affair with Lady Penelope, or whatever her name is. He said it had made divorcing his wife easier and speedier. The man is shameless.

This is the man who, when he was caught sucking the toes of bit-part actress Antonia de Sancha, persuaded his wife to be photographed smiling beside him and announce to the world that she was standing by her man. The man who even wheeled out his unfortunate in-laws to pose for family photos in a blatant attempt to salvage his political career. I can remember writing at the time that his mother-in-law, poor woman, had an expression on her face which made her look as if a dog was pissing up her leg. Which in a way was exactly what was happening.

He had no qualms at the last election posing with his wife and children and banging on about family values. It was he who put his unfortunate relatives in the spotlight, not the newspapers. And yet he has the gall to complain about Press intrusion and, when he was National Heritage Secretary, warned newspapers that they were 'drinking in the Last Chance saloon'. He is quite clearly a man with no shame, no manners and no respect for anyone. It is his brazen opportunism which appals me most. You'll find a list of his consultancies and directorships listed in the chapter 'Snouts In The Trough'. For instance, does anybody seriously believe that Mellor's services as a PR consultant to a lottery company would have been in demand had he been a bingo caller in Putney rather than the ex-Minister for Lotteries?

You can understand why the lobby companies would want to try and buy his influence. But I've never properly been able to understand why television and radio producers fawn all over him, why the *Guardian* gives him a column, filled with self-aggrandising rubbish, and how he became Radio Personality of the Year in 1995. Who voted for this patronising creep? It is impossible to turn on the telly without being confronted with his smug mug. Switch on the wireless and there he is pontificating on everything from Scunthorpe United's relegation prospects to the Meaning of Life.

After his enforced exit from the Cabinet – following the exposure of his toe-sucking, free-loading exploits – a discreet period of silence might have been in order. Quite the opposite, in fact. Mellor's proudest boast is the amount of money he has made from writing and broadcasting since he stopped being Minister of Free Tickets. He was pictured at the beginning of 1995 inspecting a house in Docklands on the market for £1.3 million.

Despite shamelessly cashing in on his sleazy celebrity, he is trying to cast himself in the role of noble victim. Exhibiting classic delusions of grandeur symptoms, he compared himself to nineteenth-century Prime Ministers Lord Palmerston and William Gladstone, two notorious political swordsmen. They got away with it, he argued, so why shouldn't he? Well, for a start, they wouldn't have got away with it today. And anyway – how shall I put it? – Mister, you're no Lord Palmerston.

In one interview, Mellor reiterated his contempt for the Press and explained why he thinks people find him arrogant. He says he was singled out because he was different from some of the other faceless berks in the Cabinet. 'I would have had a far easier ride if I was one of those interchangeable men in suits.' But if Mellor was that outstanding, why did his friend John Major give him such a Mickey Mouse job instead of installing him in one of the great offices of state? And as for being different, he does have a point. He is indeed different from most of his colleagues. They don't, as a general rule, cheat on their wives with gruesome old slappers like Antonia de Sancha. They don't all deceive their constituents. Well, not in that sense. They don't all take free holidays from the blonde daughters of terrorist paymasters, or sponge off rich businessmen. And if they do get caught out, they fade quietly into the background and keep their heads down for a decent interval. Cecil Parkinson springs to mind.

In the end I worked out why editors and producers indulge him and why my journalistic colleagues beat a path to his door. Mellor is deceiving himself if he thinks he is in demand because of his dazzling wit, or razor-sharp intellect, his dashing good looks, or his encyclopaedic knowledge of lower-division football. He is wheeled out for our amusement, so we can all point our fingers and laugh at him. 'Look, it's that ugly MP who was caught with that toe-sucking bow-wow, Anthea whats'ername. You know, that grisly-looking bird on "Wogan" the other night. I wondered what happened to him.' The former Minister of Fun is making an appropriate contribution to the nation, as an exhibit in a freak show.

Roll up, roll up. Come see The Mellorphant Man.

Channel 4 offered Mellor his own chat show. He turned it down – you'll like this – because he refused to ask people questions about their private lives. I tried to imagine what the programme would have been like.

opening music

Melly the Mellorphant
Packed his trunk
And said goodbye to his missus
Of he went with a big fat wad
And someone else's wife

wild canned applause

MELLOR: Hello, good evening, and that'll be ten grand. Will you please welcome my first guest. She's a talented actress, so please put your hands together for Antonia de Sancha. (*Enter Antonia*). Lovely to have you see me again, Antonia. Tell me, what have you been doing lately?

ANTONIA: Absolutely nothing, thanks to you.

MELLOR: I've been very busy myself. I've got this chat show, a radio show, a column in the *Guardian* and a new classy bit of stuff.

ANTONIA: Bastard!

MELLOR: I suppose a toe-job's out of the question? (*Antonia tips glass of water over Mellor and exits stage left.*) My next guest is another lovely lady. We last saw her posing astride a rocking horse. Will you please welcome Mona Bauwens. (*Enter Mona, dressed in the uniform of the PLO.*) Have you brought the money? (*Mona hands over fat brown envelope.*) That's a lovely tan you've got there. Have you been on holiday?

MONA: As a matter of fact, I've just spent two weeks in Spain.

MELLOR: Why didn't you invite me?

MONA: Look what happened last time.

MELLOR: I blame the Press.

MONA: You make me puke.

 Mona exits stage right.

MELLOR: And now, please welcome my next guest, another beauty, the lovely Lady Cobham. (*Enter Lady Cobham.*) Did I leave my razor in the bathroom, darling?

LADY COBHAM: Yes, and you forgot to flush the toilet again.

MELLOR: Sorry, darling. My wife always used to do that for me.

LADY COBHAM: What did your last servant die of?

MELLOR: Embarrassment.

LADY COBHAM: Well, if you think I'm going to be your skivvy, you can forget it. I'm going back to my husband. I don't know what I ever saw in you.

 Lady C dumps a pile of washing in Mellor's lap and exits.

MELLOR: My next guest is the distinguished editor of a national newspaper, from the *Guardian*, Peter Preston. (*Enter Preston.*) Why didn't you publish my last column?

PRESTON: Because it was attacking newspapers which use underhand methods to expose crooked and hypocritical politicians.

MELLOR: I thought it was brilliant.

PRESTON: You would.

MELLOR: But you're a member of the Press Complaints Commission.

PRESTON: Not any more, mush.

MELLOR: But the *Guardian* is always banging on about how it is wrong for newspapers to use deception.

PRESTON: Except when we do it.

MELLOR: You're as bad as all the rest of them.

PRESTON: And you're sacked.

 Exit Preston.

MELLOR: My star guest tonight is one of the most talented, handsome, debonair men on the planet. Will you please welcome . . . David Mellor! (*Produces giant mirror.*) Mirror, mirror, on the wall, who's the greatest of them all?

 Cut to mirror.

MIRROR: (*Silence.*)

MELLOR: That's enough about you, let's talk about me. (*Mirror topples over and shatters into 10,000 pieces.*) If that's your attitude, then I'm off back to my wife. I know where my bread's buttered.

HOMELY-LOOKING WOMAN IN AUDIENCE: Oh, no you're not. I've had the locks changed.

DIRECTOR: Cut!

MAN IN BEARD FROM CHANNEL 4: Looks like we're stuck with Clive Anderson.

MELLOR: When do I get paid?

MAKING A DECENT FIST OF POLITICAL CORRECTNESS

Even the deaf – sorry, the aurally challenged – have fallen victim to the all-pervasive forces of political correctness. A whole new PC sign language has been invented. It means that the deaf will not be allowed to flatten their nose to indicate someone of Afro-Caribbean origin. Instead they will have to draw the outline of Africa. This could cause some confusion. How will anyone know they're not referring to India or South America or Kate O'Mara's Triangle, for that matter? Interestingly, there is no agreed sign language for the expression 'political correctness'.

Ever anxious to help, I have devised a suitable gesture to indicate political correctness, which can be employed by both the deaf and those without hearing difficulties. It is very simple to learn and should be employed at all times whenever describing the politically correct.

There are five easy steps:

1 Form your right hand into a loose fist, as if you are holding an imaginary broom handle.
2 Put your thumb and forefinger together to form an O shape.
3 Crook your wrist.
4 Vigorously move your lower arm up and down for at least ten seconds.
5 Repeat.

WE ARE NOT ABUSED

Just occasionally some good ideas come out of America. I am increasingly coming around to the idea that what we need in this country is more direct action and more civil disobedience. We should begin to follow the example of Middle America, which is at last fighting back against the forces of political correctness, especially the burgeoning child 'abuse' industry.

I took heart from the case of a tired and exasperated mother who slapped her insolent nine-year-old son in a Georgia shopping mall and was reported to police by an outraged shop assistant. She was arrested, handcuffed and led away to jail where she was charged and warned that she could face up to twenty years behind bars for assault and child abuse. The boy admitted that he was being 'bratty' and thoroughly deserved his punishment. His mother snapped when he called his sister a 'bitch' – an offence for which, in other circumstances, feminists would be demanding castration. My experience of American children is that generally they are spoilt, tyrannical monsters who would all benefit from being slapped daily as a matter of routine. Otherwise they will grow up to become tyrannical, monstrous adults like the supermarket assistant who shopped this unfortunate harassed mother.

In America, slapping a child is now obviously considered

even more serious than sexist language, a trend which will inevitably develop in Britain and which has already manifested itself in the wave of hysteria generated by Esther Rantzen's Childline and the confiscation of thousands of children by social workers. Soon the jails will be filled with parents found guilty of sending naughty children to their rooms in contravention of the Child Protection Act. There are, however, encouraging signs of a backlash in redneck Georgia. Customers of the supermarket which employs this appalling copper's nark demonstrated their disgust by filling trolleys with frozen food and leaving them to thaw in aisles.

Let's hope this kind of direct action also spreads to Britain. Only a concerted campaign of civil disobedience will roll back the engulfing tide of political correctness and derail the burgeoning family persecution industry. We could start by sending cases of rotting fish to Rochdale social services.

SLEAZE TEST

Every time a politician is involved in a sexual or financial scandal, there are those who urge us to be more understanding. 'MPs are just like everyone else. It's not fair to judge them differently,' is the cry. Try this simple test. Pick 300 men at random from any walk of life. Then answer these questions. Has any of them recently:

1 Fathered children by a woman to whom he is not married or with whom he is not living?
2 Shared a bed with another man on a holiday to France?
3 Had a wife who shot herself because her husband was having an affair?
4 Used his employer's money to pay his private legal fees or has been overdrawn on his credit card?
5 Been caught lying to his employers and got away with it?
6 Taken free holidays from the daughter of a PLO paymaster?
7 Had five mistresses?
8 Made love to a bit-part actress while wearing a Chelsea strip?
9 Been accused of gerrymandering or profiting from council house sales?
10 Been alleged to like dressing up in French maids' outfits and have cream buns thrown at him?
11 Been linked to three-in-a-bed sessions with bisexual Nigerian footballers?

12 Been found dead wearing nothing but stockings, suspenders, electric flex and a bin-liner, with a satsuma stuffed in his mouth?

If you answer yes to none of the above, you keep blameless company.

If you answer yes to one, don't worry — we've all been overdrawn on our credit card.

If you answer yes to between two and four, never mind, nobody's perfect.

If your Biro has run out, you can only be a Tory MP.

NANNY KNOWS BEST

It wouldn't be so bad if it was only the state which wanted to nanny and police us. But more and more employers are getting in on the act. There are widespread no-smoking bans in all offices, dress codes, no-beard rules, no drinking at lunchtime, no eating crisps.

It's one thing laying down rules of behaviour during office hours. After all, if an employer is paying someone good money to represent his company, he is entitled to insist upon certain standards, although if there had been a no-drinking at lunchtime policy applied to what we used to call Fleet Street, there would not be a single paper in the country published. But more on the newspaper industry in a moment.

First let us consider one of the last great state concerns, British Rail – currently in the process of being broken up for privatisation. BR was the first organisation to introduce random breath tests for staff – set at half the legal limit for driving a car. If employees register more than thirty milligrams of alcohol in their blood – compared to a driving limit of eighty – they face disciplinary action, including the sack. Fair enough. You can understand BR being anxious to ensure that drivers and guards and other safety-related staff don't report for work under the influence of alcohol. But this rule doesn't just apply to engine drivers and other operational staff. It also applies to typists, clerks and managers – and to my mind is an outrageous infringement of civil liberties. No one wants their staff falling over after lunch. But under BR's tough rules, a swift pint can be enough to put you over the top. And BR also said it was planning to breathalyse people when they arrive at work first thing in the morning – an outrageous and impertinent attempt to dictate what employees do in their own time. Furthermore, if someone is considered by law to be sober enough to drive a car at 70mph, why the hell are they thought to be too drunk to drive a British Rail photocopier?

When the rule was first introduced, the *Sunday Telegraph* breath-tested commuters at London's Victoria station on Friday morning. Most of them failed, but all of them were perfectly fit for work. If they had been on the BR payroll, they could well have found themselves out of a job by the time the pubs opened.

This sort of nonsense is entirely consistent with an organisation which has lost the plot completely. If BR spent half as much time making sure the trains ran on time as it does dreaming up bloody stupid rules to stop staff taking a small schooner of sherry of an evening, then perhaps it wouldn't have to be privatised. Throughout the public sector, organisations are dictating to their employees how they should behave in their own time.

A number of local authorities have now followed the lead of the Pembrokeshire Health Authority, which announced that staff would be banned from smoking even if they were off-duty – with the full support of Conservative ministers who claim to be champions of individual liberty. You have been warned. But if you think it is only in state industries, Town Halls and government departments that people create unnecessary jobs for themselves and eventually take leave of their senses, then you're wrong. Exactly the same thing happens in industry. Instead of calling themselves outreach co-ordinators, this bunch of supernumeraries call themselves 'human resources professionals' and busy themselves enforcing 'employee well-being enhancement schemes' and 'safety' programmes – which always amount to stopping people doing things like going for a pint at lunchtime and wandering from one part of the workplace to another without a Man From Uncle security code.

Which brings us back to the newspaper industry – and Wapping. News International set up a Human Resources Committee, presumably to make up for denying trades union recognition. I never worked out how you got elected to this grand-sounding body, but everyone on it seemed to have the mentality of Reg Hollis in 'The Bill'. The employees on the committee seemed more keen to impose draconian rules and regulations on the staff than did the management. I decided it was time to go freelance when the committee bombarded noticeboards with a warning about the dangers of sunbathing. It's enough to drive you to drink.

PAY AS YOU BURN

Every once in a while another survey is published which 'proves' that most people are happy to pay more. All I can say is that 'most people' are liars. Whatever they tell opinion pollsters, the truth is that 'most people' hate paying taxes. Why do you think the Tories are primarily so unpopular? It is because, despite being the party of so-called 'low taxation', the tax burden on the average family is even higher than it was under Denis Healey in Jim Callaghan's Labour government in 1979. In fact, if 'most people' had any idea of exactly how much tax they do pay, there would be riots in the street. That's why the Inland Revenue invented Pay As You Earn and there is so much talk about 'take-home' pay. It is designed to deflect attention from the amount of money the State steals from the average wage packet.

Every year some organisation or other – I forget which – calculates how many days we work for the government each year. It turns out most people don't earn anything for themselves or their families until the middle of May. If you're paying tax at forty per cent, you can push that back to midsummer. If everyone had to sit down and write a cheque for several thousand pounds to the Treasury each year there would be burning public buildings all over Britain. So PAYE was dreamt up to do it by stealth. And by the time you take into account all the other taxes – VAT, council tax, etc – most of us spend at least two-thirds of the year working for the government.

It is not often the Liberals come up with a good idea. But credit where it is due. Paddy Pantsdown has suggested 'hypothecating' certain taxes, so that we know where the money we contribute is actually spent. For instance, 1p on income tax to be devoted exclusively to education. That sounds an attractive idea, but it will never be adopted. Politicians and civil servants know we would be absolutely horrified if we found out exactly where the money went. That's one of the reasons they talk about 'resources' and 'funding' instead of 'money'. They try to kid us it's not really our hard-earned they're throwing down the gurgler. Especially if they were forced to be more specific than just '1p for education' or '2p for the police' and so on. Can you imagine what a blow-by-blow account of where the money goes would actually look like? If 'hypothecation' was adopted and public spending was itemised then your average weekly tax bill might look like this.

- Greedy and bone-idle bureaucrats sitting around picking their noses all day – £50
- Random breath tests – £1.50
- New cars for NHS managers – £6
- Artificial insemination for lesbians – 75p
- Outreach co-ordinators (misc) – £10
- Golliwog inspectors – 50p
- Lazy Greek farmers – £2
- Surly Spanish fishermen – £1.75
- Italian crooks – £2.50
- Traffic humps – £4
- People with beards telling you how many potatoes to eat each week – £3.50
- New homes in Holland Park for Eritreans – £1.20
- Gerry Adams' legal bill – 45p

- Compensation to Winston Silcott – £1.40
- Lorry-loads of paper being shunted all over Europe – £2
- Neil and Glenys Kinnock – 20p
- Lies about AIDS – £1.20
- Buggering up the town centre – £4.50
- Refusing to empty the dustbins and scattering litter all over the street once a week – 75p
- Sending Councillor and Mrs Bloggs on a fact-finding mission to the Bahamas – 30p
- Windsurfing holidays for horrible hooligans who mug old ladies, burgle your house and steal your car radio – £1.65
- Fatuous leaflets from the DTI – 65p
- Prosecuting members of the Women's Institute for making jam – 25p
- Putting 200-year-old family firms out of business for not having enough sinks in the toilet – £1.10
- Hundreds of thousands of people generally making a bloody nuisance of themselves – £25

WE DON'T NEED NO EDUKASHON

When I was at school the teachers all wore tweed sports jackets with leather patches on the sleeves, cavalry twill trousers, highly-polished hand-stitched brogues and smoked pipes. And that was just the women. There were one or two we suspected of not being like other men, especially the sadistic games master who delighted in flicking our shrivelled willies with a wet towel as we ran from the freezing showers after an hour and a half of male bonding on the rugby pitch. But short of clambering on the five-speed, drop-handlebar Raleigh racing bikes we got for passing the eleven-plus, following his Ford Corsair 2000E back to his Tudorbethan semi and setting up twenty-four-hour surveillance, there was no way we could discover what he got up to in his private life. OK, so we knew he played cricket for the Old Boys' XI on a Sunday and was partial to Louis Armstrong and Fats Waller and had a penchant for Rinstead pastilles. But that was about it. It was the same with all the teachers. There were rumours, of course. The walls of the ablutions served as a noticeboard for the latest theories about the love lives of Miss X and Mr Y. And everyone knew what happened on the school trip, didn't they? But I suppose we really thought that teachers were a bit like our parents. They didn't actually do it. They were far too old.

If we knew nothing about their love lives, we knew even less about their political opinions. None of us had the faintest idea what Sir thought about the war in Vietnam, the seamen's strike, Barbara Castle's trades union legislation, nuclear weapons, the homosexual age of consent, comprehensive education, Aboriginal land rights, the Common Market, Harold Wilson or the price of Spangles. I did spot the history teacher out canvassing for the Liberals during the local council elections, but since he wore corduroy trousers, had long sideburns and once turned up in sandals it came as no surprise. No one had the faintest idea what the Liberals stood for in those days. Neither did they, apparently, except that they all knew they didn't stand for what the Tories and the Labour Party stood for. A bit like today, actually. If any of the teachers ever went on the Aldermaston march or attended a Conservative Party conference, it was not anything they ever felt they needed to share with us. They taught us what they were paid to teach us, whether maths, history or geography. They stuck to the curriculum. It was their job to impart knowledge from one generation to another, to ensure continuity. It was an almost sacred trust. If the English master had ever refused to teach Shakespeare on the grounds that it was 'blatantly heterosexist' he would have been clearing his locker before you could say Goodbye Mr Chips.

Which brings us to Miss Jane Brown, the Hackney headmistress who in 1994 banned her pupils from attending a performance of *Romeo and Juliet*, being staged specially for schools. Sadlers Wells Theatre had obtained a subsidy to enable children from the underprivileged inner-city to breathe some culture; to take them away from the drab tower-block existence and their graffiti-splattered precincts and expose them to a world of escapism and magic. Miss Brown told the theatre's management that she considered

Romeo and Juliet to be 'blatantly heterosexist' and therefore unsuitable for the children in her charge. Before I saw the photographs of Miss Brown, I could have painted you a picture –sour face, severe haircut, no make-up, shapeless boiler suit, Doc Martens. When the first snaps of Miss Brown did appear in the newspapers, it transpired that I had only forgotten the donkey jacket. Subsequently we learned that she had banned the celebration of Christmas at the school – on the grounds that it discriminated against children from the ethnic minorities – and refused to let pupils call male teachers 'Sir'. It came as no great surprise to discover that she was a lesbian with a reputation for snogging with her partner in public. A pound to a penny she is also in favour of lowering the homosexual age of consent to sixteen, positive discrimination, vegetarianism, anti-smoking, anti-vivisection, anti-nuclear and probably thinks all men are rapists. That is her prerogative. She can believe that the moon is made of green cheese, the earth is flat, babies come from behind gooseberry bushes and that one day Swindon Town will win the league and cup double. I couldn't care less how she votes, whether she went to Greenham Common, what she thinks about the testing of cosmetics on gerbils, fund-holding GPs, the rainforest, the government of Uruguay, the famine in the Sudan or the plight of Rwandan refugees. If she wishes to stand outside Sainsbury's every Saturday morning selling the *Socialist Worker* and collecting names on a Meat Is Murder petition, that is entirely a matter for her. I just don't want her bringing her prejudices into the classroom.

By all accounts, Miss Brown is an excellent teacher. But she is apparently incapable of separating her educational duties from her own political agenda. And that is what makes her – and others like her – unfit to be running our schools. We send our children to school to be educated, not indoctrinated. Miss Brown is what you get when you recruit staff from the *Guardian* jobs pages – which I discuss at length in another chapter. It seems that when it comes to hiring staff in the public sector, the ability to chant the mantras of political correctness comes before the ability actually to do the job.

I've singled out the *Romeo and Juliet* case, but could equally have chosen from dozens of others, from Norfolk to Haringey – where school libraries have been filled with books promoting homosexuality. In Halstead, in Essex – of all counties – a woman calling herself an 'infant co-ordinator' installed a Mother Christmas at the Holy Trinity Primary School. According to the headmistress this was in line with the principles of teaching feminism to five-year-olds. Next year, *Single Parent Goose* will be the school panto. In Islington, north London, a production of *Peter Pan* for schoolchildren had to proceed without Tinkerbell because education chiefs thought that any reference to 'fairies' would be offensive to homosexuals. I am not making this up. In Lewisham, south London, pre-school playgroups were banned from celebrating Christmas. This was in response to a circular from the pre-school play-groups association, which said equal emphasis should be given to Muslim and Hindu festivals.

I could go on, but I digress slightly. The main purpose of this chapter is to examine the kind of education our children are getting in state schools these days and discover what kind of people are teaching them. There appears to be a broad consensus that teaching standards have fallen and that children are less literate and numerate than they were when I left school in 1970. Employers regularly complain that job applicants can barely read and write these days. All this makes great newspaper headlines. It is true that there have been great changes in schools. We no longer have teaching by rote, there is not the emphasis on good grammar and spelling, on times tables, on basic geography. I'm not entirely convinced, however, that everything has changed for the worse. There have always been the illiterate and the innumerate. Mostly they got jobs writing public information signs for British Rail and the London Underground or went into manual employment or the Treasury, where they were put in charge of working out the Public Sector Borrowing Requirement. I can only speak from my own experience of putting two children through the state education system. They are both bright, well balanced and better qualified than I was after five years at grammar school. There have been gaps in their education, just as there were in mine. But both are literate and numerate, have a command of foreign languages and a reasonable appreciation of how many beans make five. This is not to say that their education has been perfect. But is any education? I'm not being complacent, believe me.

After a routine visit to my daughter's school and a conversation with one of her tutors which might just as well have been conducted in Flowerpot Man – no known language, during which he talked about the 'specialisms' she would be taking in her A-level course – I began to panic. Racked with middle-class guilt, I took her along to an independent schools assessment centre to try to gauge her level of attainment. The centre is funded by the private sector and its primary job is to act as a recruitment centre for fee-paying schools. I'd just joined the *Sun* and thought about investing some of my new-found riches in my daughter's education. She spent three days being tested on every subject. At the end of it all, the principal told us that apart from below-average marks in maths, she was pretty much where they would have expected a girl of her age to be. I asked if there was any point in sending her to a private school at that stage or paying for extra tuition. The principal said that I'd be better off putting the money on a horse in the 3.15 at Aintree. Private school would be a complete waste of time and while tuition might help gee her up, children would only learn if they wanted to. If she wasn't interested in maths, I could get Pythagoras himself round for a couple of hours each evening and it wouldn't make the slightest difference. I thanked her, coughed up ninety quid, and remarked that she must get hundreds of parents like me through her doors – mums and dads who have sent their children to state schools and then begun to panic as more and more of their friends have opted to send their offspring to private schools in the face of yet another report about plummeting educational standards and more depressing footage of the NUT conference, of which more shortly. Not at all, she remarked. Only about five per cent of parents she saw had children in state schools. The rest, the overwhelming majority, were spending a small fortune on private education yet were deeply unhappy about the results. So what was the point in shelling out thousands every year on school fees? I asked her. In educational terms, she explained, very little.

Why bother, then? Apparently most people do it for the uniforms, the discipline, the smaller class sizes and the extra-curricular activities – sports, drama, music, which the teaching unions in the state sector have been tending to boycott in recent years. The exam results are always more impressive, largely because the pupils sent to private schools in the first place tend to come from better-educated, more affluent families, with parents who take an intense interest in the education of their children and insist on homework coming before 'Home and Away' and glue-sniffing. But the most compelling reason parents sacrifice foreign holidays and new motors to foot the school fees bill

is to keep their sons and daughters away from the Jane
Browns of this world. One look at the NUT conference is
enough to scare any parent into holding up a sub-post office
with a sawn-off Purdey to raise the money for a place at
Eton – or St Trinian's, for that matter – just to keep his kids
out of the clutches of the forces of political correctness.

The NUT conference is not about education. The 1994
gathering at Scarborough was like walking through a time
tunnel to the Labour conferences of the late 1970s and early
1980s – screaming, scruffy Trots, calling for boycotts of
this, non-co-operation with that, strikes over this, go-
slows over that, Maggie Maggie Maggie, Out Out Out,
except in this case it was Major Major Major, Out Out Out.
Delegates were more concerned with bringing down the
government than teaching children to read and write.
However distorted the picture painted of teachers by the
NUT conference, the public image of Mr Chips is not
Captain Pugwash lookalike Doug McEvoy in his sober
suit, but a greasy, unkempt hooligan called Kev with an
SWP banner in one hand and a copy of *Militant* in the other,
hell-bent on using Britain's playgrounds as a political
battleground. Too many teachers seem to see education in
terms of social engineering.

Opposition has centred on government attempts to bring
in testing at regular intervals. In typical fashion, the first
tests were cumbersome and involved mountains of paperwork. What else should we expect from the bureaucrats at
the Department of Education? But these problems have
now been sorted out. Testing need not be difficult. When I
was at school, we were tested every week on spelling and
arithmetic. It wouldn't take long for a teacher to mark a
simple paper and record the results. All the government
required for seven-year-olds was that they know the
alphabet and could read aloud thirty common words. It

can't be all that difficult. By the time he was three, my son could repeat off by heart the words: 'Brown, Baker, Henry, Blanchflower, Norman, Mackay, Jones, White, Smith, Allen, Dyson'. But what the activists in the NUT object to is testing *per se*. Because those really being tested are the teachers. And they are worried that their own incompetence and inadequacy would be exposed. At one teaching conference, a headmistress from Rotherham was given a standing ovation when she insisted she would rather break the law than force pupils to sit a test which made them cry. Silly cow. 4B must see her as a soft touch.

That gets to the heart of the whole debate about self-expression – the idea that kids learn more by sticking their hands in a bucket of play-dough and pretending to be a tree than by reading Richmal Crompton or Shakespeare. For some reason or other, the thinking today is that lessons have to be 'fun'. Whoever said that school was meant to be a barrel of laughs? It can be bloody hard work, like life. If children aren't forced to take spelling tests which make them cry, is it any wonder they end up sitting in shop doorways behind a makeshift cardboard sign reading: '*Hungrey, homles and jobles*'. What teachers really mean when they say they want lessons to be more interesting is more interesting for *them*. It must be pretty dull listening to year after year of snotty-nosed kids chanting 'One two is two, two twos are four, three twos are six' for most of your working life. But teaching, like all jobs, involves routine and drudgery. The best teachers acknowledge that. In that respect teaching is no different from most other walks of life. Can you imagine if bus drivers decided to vary their routine every day, ostensibly to make life more interesting for the passengers, and never took the same route twice. No one would ever know where the bloody hell they were.

Teaching should be a vocation, not just a job.

Somewhere between me leaving school and my children starting, we lost the plot. The profession became devalued. I've never been entirely sure of the sequence of events which led to this. Did teachers become militant malcontents because successive governments forgot their worth and allowed their pay to drift downwards? Or did they become devalued because of the antics of Kev and his pals? Whatever the cause, the figures show that in 1974, when professional pay scales were established in schools, teachers were paid 37 per cent above the average white-collar salary. By 1991, when the exercise was carried out again, teachers' pay had fallen to 1 per cent *less*. The calibre of those attracted into the profession was bound to fall as a result. I know one primary school deputy head – a married man with children – who fits carpets in his spare time to make ends meet. This is spare time which a few years ago he would happily have devoted to running the school football team or organising the fête. When I saw him last he was thinking of taking up carpet fitting full-time. And another good teacher bites the dust. Into this poorly-paid void have drifted the otherwise unemployable dregs of the poly-technocracy, life's full-time students who look upon the staff room as an extension of the NUS common room – a cosy, subsidised cocoon with little work and long holidays and endless opportunities for making mischief and playing Che Guevara.

Looking at the Wolfie Smiths bouncing up and down on the rostrum in the Scarborough Winter Gardens, I couldn't help wondering who else would give them a job. There's not a lot of call for bitter and twisted revolutionaries in the insurance or double-glazing industries. Our children deserve better. In the long run, teachers will have to be paid more, will have to have their proper status restored. But that will not be achieved simply by increasing their wages.

They will have to earn the respect of society by putting pupils before politics and leaving their prejudices behind when they pass through the school gates. Oh, and a return to tweed jackets might just be a start.

Teachers only teach what they are told to teach. The ultimate responsibility lies with the government, local authorities and the teacher training colleges. Teacher training colleges seem to take the Shavian principle of 'He who can, does. He who cannot, teaches' one step beyond. Shaw forgot to add: 'Those who can't teach, teach teachers.' Town Halls, regardless of which party is nominally in power, are staffed and controlled by a self-perpetuating, politically-correct clique, needless to say recruited from the jobs pages of the *Guardian*. So it's no good looking to them to safeguard traditional teaching standards. You might just as well ask Michael Jackson to babysit.

With this is mind, in 1988 the Conservative government introduced the Education Reform Act, designed to introduce a compulsory national curriculum intended to guarantee consistent minimum standards across the country and combat the idea that the 3Rs meant 'Racism, Resources and Revolution'. The day I began this chapter, the committee set up to make recommendations on history teaching published its report, just two months after the then education secretary John Patten had spoken of the need to prevent schools 'robbing children of their birthright of knowledge about our country's history'.

Now you and I might have thought that a basic history of the British might include the Roman Settlement, Henry VIII, the Gunpowder Plot, Nelson, Richard the Lionheart and the Crusades, Clive of India, the Magna Carta, the Great Fire of London, the Peasants' Revolt, the Zulu and Napoleonic Wars, Florence Nightingale, Marlborough and

Winston Churchill as well as the development of British democracy and the Welfare State. Apparently not. The committee, under Sir Ron Dearing, former chairman of the Post Office, did not prescribe any of the above, deciding instead to make them merely optional. And we wonder why the only post which ever seems to arrive on time is junk mail. The government would have been better off putting Postman Pat in charge. Not a single British monarch is included and the only battle required to be taught is the Battle of Hastings. You might have thought the Battle of Britain was worth a passing mention. So what did Sir Ron's committee consider essential history for British schoolchildren? 'Everyday life' in Roman Britain, 'everyday life' in Anglo-Saxon Britain, 'everyday life' in Viking Britain, 'changes in town and countryside life between 1500–1750'. Fair enough, you might say. But what about 'a study of past non-European society, including the everyday lives (*those everyday lives again*) of men and women' chosen from a list including the Indus valley, Mesopotamia, Benin and the Aztecs. Or 'a unit involving the study of people from a non-European background in a past society . . . over a long period of time, e.g. Islamic civilisations, the civilisations of Peru, Black peoples of the Americas' and 'the social, cultural, religious and ethnic diversity of the societies studied'. All compulsory. You might ask yourself how all this happened under a Conservative government which cuts its suits from the Union Flag and worships at Winston's altar. Questions on a postcard to Conservative Central Office, Smith Square, London SW1. Even the British history prescribed by the committee is based not on fact but on opinion. Children would not be taught what actually happened, but academics' interpretations of what happened and why it happened, complete with attempts to 'relate' the lot of a twelfth-century serf to the 'everyday life' of someone living half-way up a tower block in Salford. What is conspicuously absent is any sense of civilisation and national pride.

I sometimes wonder whether those responsible for our schools hate the country in which they were born and are ashamed of its achievements. You don't have to glory in blood and guts and death and destruction to acknowledge the heroic sacrifice of the pilots who fought in the Battle of Britain – or vote Tory to appreciate Churchill's role in saving Britain from defeat and occupation. You can be assured of one thing: there'd be no Anti-Nazi League if Hitler had won the war.

The educational establishment seems to have been infiltrated by the kind of nutters running riot in the United States, who deride anything by a Dead White European Male as worthless and elevate ancient Namibian finger painting to quasi-religious status. Somehow the view has got around that all cultures are equal, all art is equal, and that African art is more pure and 'relevant' than anything knocked up during the Renaissance. This is patent nonsense. Is a mud hut really 'equal' to the Sistine chapel? Is a crude wood carving from the Limpopo really as valuable and accomplished as a Da Vinci sculpture or a Constable landscape? Are jungle drums 'equal' to Beethoven, or 'Roll Over Beethoven' for that matter? There is an obsession with the modern phenomenon of 'cultural, social and ethnic' history, which seeks to pretend that the Aborigines have given as much to the world as Western Europe – despite the fact that when the first white settlers arrived in Australia the Aborigines hadn't even invented the wheel. There is the assumption that anything overtly Anglo-Saxon is racist. It leads to the kind of madness which saw a Birmingham headmaster, Don Ablett, revise teaching of the alphabet so as not to offend Muslims. He decided to ban the phrase 'P is for Pig' because Islamic pupils might be upset. Out went 'P is for Pig'. In came 'P is for Panda'. I'm surprised he didn't make it 'P is for Panda Car', a concept most inner-city Brummie kids would grasp instantly.

To be honest, I couldn't care less whether 'P is for Pig' or 'P is for Poppadam', just as long as they don't grow up thinking 'P is for Cat'. When the story broke, around the time of the Gulf War, I devised a politically-correct alphabet – specially tailored not to offend Muslim pupils – to be used in primary schools throughout the country:

A is for Ayatollah
B is for Baghdad
C is for Curry
D is for Djellaba
E is for Emir
F is for Fatwa
G is for Gaddafi
H is for Hizbollah
I is for Intifada
J is for Jihad
K is for Khomeini
L is for Lebanon
M is for Mecca
N is for Nan
O is for Onion Bhaji
P is for Palestine
Q is for Q8
R is for Rushdie
S is for Saddam
T is for Teheran
U is for United Arab Emirates
V is for Vindaloo
W is for Western Imperialist Aggressor
X is for Xenophobia
Y is for Yasser Arafat
Z is for Zionist Running Dog of The Great Satan.

I wonder if the government might like to include it in the next national curriculum?

Eventually it was announced that a compromise had been reached on the new curriculum. The syllabus would attempt to make lessons more relevant to children growing up in the 1990s, presumably concentrating more on 'every-day life'. I managed to obtain a sample exam for eleven-year–olds. All questions are multiple choice. Time allowed: 30 minutes.

MATHEMATICS

Question One

If it takes two boys fifteen minutes to burgle a maisonette, how long will it take one boy to mug an old lady?

1 10 seconds.

2 10 minutes.

3 Depends on whether the old bag puts up a struggle.

Question Two

If a car radio costs £150 in Halfords, £120 in Dixons and £10 in the back bar of the Dog and Duck, how much can you save by?

1 Buying it in Dixons.

2 Buying it in the Dog and Duck.

3 Nicking it yourself.

Question Three

If a man is fined £1000 for smoking on a London bus and another man is fined £2500 for driving at 85mph on a deserted motorway, what will be the penalty for a joyrider who steals a car, drives it through a tobacconist's window and steals 20,000 Silk Cut?

1 £10.

2 £100.

3 Two months' windsurfing in the Bahamas and £500 spending money.

Question Four

If a Chief Constable employs 500 officers to police a Wednesday night football match in the Vauxhall Conference and a further 700 on setting up road blocks to check tax discs and mount random tyre tread checks, how many officers will he send to investigate a burglary at your home?

1 1.

2 2.

3 None.

SCIENCE

Question One

You have one gram of cocaine. Describe the most effective way of turning it into 1000 individual deals of crack.

1 Cut it with baking soda under laboratory conditions.

2 Roll your dealer.

3 Snort the lot and forget what the question was.

Question Two

It is Friday night but your Ecstasy dealer has been intercepted by the drug squad. You have only £10 with which to get rat-faced. Describe the most scientific method of doing this:

1 Eight cans of Special Brew.

2 One half-bottle of Bell's and a carrier bag full of Bostik.

3 Buy a knife, hold up an off-licence and drink as much as you like.

Question Three

You are setting off for an evening's ram-raiding. Using proper scientific criteria, describe the ideal performance and safety characteristics of the vehicle:

1 0–60 in eight seconds.
2 Driver's side airbag.
3 None, provided it belongs to someone else.

BRITISH HISTORY

Question One

The Prince of Wales is?

1 A prince who lives in Wales.
2 Heir to the throne of the United Kingdom.
3 A pub off the East Lancs Road.

Question Two

The estranged wife of the Prince of Wales comes from a wealthy family with a home at Althorp, in Northamptonshire. Was her name before she married?

1 Diana Spencer.
2 Frank Spencer.
3 Tracy Spencer.
4 Spencer Tracy.

Question Three

It is now widely accepted that the Second World War was won by a handful of Native Americans and a battalion of Ghurkas. Who was the Nazi war criminal responsible for millions of deaths who started it all?

1 Derek Beackon.
2 Winston Churchill.
3 General Patton.
4 John Patten.

BIOLOGY

Question One

You are a girl of fifteen being pressured to sleep with your boyfriend, even though you know you might get pregnant. Do you?

1 Say No because you are under age.
2 Go on the Pill.
3 Put your name down for a council house.

Question Two

It is now accepted that AIDS is the greatest threat to the human race. What is the best way to prevent it spreading?

1 Always use a condom.
2 Don't inject heroin or have anal sex with promiscuous homosexuals and sub-Saharan Africans.
3 Spend hundreds of millions of pounds on outreach co-ordinators and a wholly misleading advertising campaign aimed at heterosexuals.
4 Tie a red ribbon round the old oak tree.

HOME ECONOMICS

Question One

Using your skill and judgement, describe and prepare a simple meal for a single-parent family of four. Choose from:

1 Mince beef, carrots, cabbage and new potatoes and a pot of tea.
2 Pop-Tarts, Pot-Noodles, prawn cocktail flavour crisps and Sainsbury's Cola.
3 The Pizza-To-Go Dial-A-Dinner delivery service, extra toppings 50p.

Question Two

It is the middle of winter. You have just received your social security Giro for the next two weeks. The gas is about to be cut off, the children need new clothes and the pantry is bare. Do you?

1 Pay the gas bill.
2 Buy the children some warm winter clothes and stock up on soups, eggs and vegetables.
3 Go down the pub, get legless, rent a video and put the rest on the 3.15 at Wincanton.

SPORT
(compulsory)

Students must pick at least one sport from the following list approved by the National Union of Teachers.

1 Nintendo.
2 Darts.
3 Dog Fighting.
4 Fantasy Football.

ARTS AND CRAFTS

Describe the ideal use for a Stanley knife.

1 Preparing mortice joints in the construction of a simple bookshelf.
2 Carving a replica of an African tribal mask.
3 Slashing the face of a Millwall fan.
4 Cutting the straps of a lady's handbag in your local Arndale Centre.

All questions must be answered in paint and sprayed on the wall of the Department of Education and Science.

THE RUBBER JOHNNY POLICE

How stupid do they think we are? Barely a day goes by without yet another nannying health and safety warning being issued by a branch of the Rubber Johnny Police. Eat this, don't eat that. Take more exercise. Don't overdo it. You're driving too fast, you're driving too slow. You mustn't drink more than twenty-one units a week. Cut down on fat, eat more greens, stop picking your nose, wash your hands after you've been to the toilet or you'll die screaming and kicking in agony and you won't go to heaven, so there.

We are paying for all this, you know. Every single penny spent on health advertisements comes out of our taxes. We are paying them to tell us what to do. Most of these advertising campaigns are statements of the bleeding obvious. They must think we are all brain damaged. Is there anyone – anyone at all – who doesn't think that cigarette smoking has some harmful side effects, including death? Last Valentine's Day, alongside a page of soppy Valentine messages in one of the Sunday papers was a facing page advertisement from the Health Education Authority. It featured a smoke ring in the shape of a heart, captioned: 'Last year 32,000 smokers died from a broken heart,' and went on to detail the dangers of smoking, of which even the dimmest person in Britain must by now be aware.

If people still choose to smoke, that is entirely a matter for them. And as for passive smoking, forget it. If you believe the figures, which I don't, there are now more people dying from passive smoking than there are from smoking itself. This is quite obviously complete nonsense. Yet we allow the health gestapo to get away with peddling lies and insulting our intelligence. In early 1995 it was announced that a group of smokers were being given £100,000 legal aid to sue the tobacco companies for not telling them that cigarettes could be harmful. Well, excuse me, but where have these chimps been for the past fifty years? My grandfather died forty-odd years ago from lung cancer. Everyone said that it was the cigarettes which killed him. When I was at school, cigarettes were nicknamed 'coffin nails' and 'cancer sticks'. Are they really trying to tell us that there are adults around who thought smoking sixty Woodbines a day was as beneficial as breathing in Alpine air all your life? No, this is lawyer-driven litigation, feeding off the greed and stupidity of a handful of gullible smokers. Once again, this has nothing to do with health or the common good and everything to do with artificial job creation and dreaming up new ways to spend our money.

There is one glaring physical manifestation of the nanny state, on the main road through the village of Great Leighs, in Essex. As you approach a series of gentle bends in the road, your concentration is interrupted by a giant, illuminated sign, flashing the message: 'Too Fast, Too Fast.' Too fast for what? Milk floats? Ferraris? Little old ladies in Morris 1000 Travellers? Chris Boardman? Surely the safe speed for negotiating a bend depends entirely on what you are driving. A curve which would present no hazard at 50mph to a BMW 325 might prove a lethal obstacle at 20mph to a fifteen-year-old Skoda. Yet someone in authority has decided to impose an arbitrary limit and wasted thousands of pounds of public money erecting this impertinent electronic monstrosity.

This is exactly the same kind of mentality as the jobsworths at the Department of Health, who issued a bossy directive on what we should eat. For instance, we are told we should all eat four and a half slices of bread a day. What sort of bread? Wrapped and sliced? Ciabatta? And why four and a half slices? Why not four slices, or even five? when it comes to fruit, we are allowed one and a half pieces a day. What are we supposed to do with the other half? Half a day-old banana is not a pretty sight. We are recommended to eat three 'egg-sized' potatoes a day. What exactly is 'egg-sized'? Gulls' eggs? Easter eggs? And why three 'egg-sized' potatoes and not one cricket ball-sized spud? Never accuse these officials of being killjoys. All wholewheat pasta and no sweeties makes Jack a dull boy, so we are allowed the occasional treat. We can choose between three-quarters of a bar of chocolate or three boiled sweets. After a couple of weeks you'd have a fridge full of odd bits of Mars Bars and rotting fruit. And when they say boiled sweets, do they mean Fox's Glacier Mints or Aniseed Twists? Do two Polos equal one gobstopper? And what happens if you fancy a finger of fudge of an evening? More to the point, at a time when the NHS is in crisis and nurses are being sacked, we shouldn't be paying bureaucrats and busybodies good money to argue about whether two-thirds of a gingernut is better for us than three-fifths of a Curly Wurly.

If the Government's plan for identity cards ever takes off, we'll probably be forced to carry details of our cholesterol levels about our person at all times. Yes, I know all the arguments about ID cards, how they are supposed to cut crime, terrorism, driving test fraud and probably indigestion and German measles, too. But don't be taken in. If we ever get identity cards, they will be used to bully, nanny and harass us by the police, government officials and assorted gollywog inspectors and muesli wardens. We are being suffocated by the State, treated as imbeciles to be herded and prodded and controlled. We are adults. We can make our own minds up about what we eat, how much we drink, how fast we approach a bend on a deserted country road. Yet in many ways we have only ourselves to blame. Half the population refuses to take any responsibility for its own actions or welfare. They want to be able to point the finger and say it's someone else's fault.

Someone else's fault if they get lung cancer from smoking.

Someone else's fault if they walk out in front of a car.

Someone else's fault if they fall down blind drunk after drinking twenty-four pints of Special Brew.

Someone else's fault if they get so fat they can't get out of their sofa because they've spent their whole life stuffing their faces with creme eggs and smokey bacon crisps. And the nanny state encourages them to think like this. If 'guidelines' identifying dangerous foods are issued by government, then it automatically follows that the manufacturers of those dangerous foods must be liable for over-indulgence. If smokers can get £100,000 out of the legal aid pot to sue the tobacco companies, can it be long before the obese get legal aid to sue fish and chip shops and the chocolate manufacturers? You might think I'm joking. But I'm deadly serious. Soon someone will be given legal aid to sue the Met Office because it's too hot.

Every summer brings new warning of skin cancer. As soon as the sun shines, out come the Rubber Johnny Police, all sirens blaring. They're like the Harry Enfield character, Mr You Don't Want To Do It Like That.

You don't want to go sunbathing, you want to stay indoors.

You don't want another pint of lager, you want a mineral water.

You don't want to have sex like that, you want to wear a condom.

You don't want to enjoy yourselves, you want to be really miserable. That's what you want to be. In the time it takes to peel off a T-shirt, the airwaves are filled with 'experts' warning that unless we put our clothes back on immediately we will all die of skin cancer. The BBC weather forecast now features a 'burn index' and skin-cancer alert warning as soon as the temperature rises above freezing. Figures from Australia and Florida are trotted out to 'prove' that skin cancer is now an even bigger killer that old age. Dire predictions of a skin-cancer epidemic sweeping Britain come thick and fast. These so-called 'experts' are allowed to spew out this garbage unchallenged by interviewers either too terrified of being seen to be politically incorrect or so bored that they simply couldn't be bothered. No one ever bothers, or dares, to point out that Australia and Florida enjoy almost continuous scorching sunshine throughout the year, whereas Britain is lucky if the temperature hits 80° half-a-dozen times a year. You might get the odd bit of sunburn, but you have about as much chance of catching skin cancer in this country as Mother Teresa has of dying of AIDS. Last summer some TV programmes had live outside broadcasts from public parks with reporters and 'experts' wrapped from head to toe in sensible clothing and standing in the shade under umbrellas to illustrate the point. All around the British public lay stretched out in the sun – stripped to the waist and sipping ice-cold beer – oblivious of their ghastly fate.

And there's a variation on the theme which involves earnest young men and women with camera crews invading pubs and beer gardens on National Drinkwise

Day and pointing disapprovingly at punters guzzling in the midday sun. This is yet another scam dreamed up by the Rubber Johnny Police to jusify their existence. The same sour-faced 'experts' are always on hand to warn us not to drink too much in the hot weather, or at any other time for that matter. They produced such startling evidence as: If you drink too much, you get drunk; if you drink too much, too often, you get ill. Arbitrary limits have been laid down with no regard to age, weight or general health. Each unit is equivalent to half a bitter or a small glass of wine. So any man who drinks more than a pint-and-a-half a day is classified as a problem drinker. There are ways round the system, which allow you to get completely rat-arsed while at the same time nominally staying within the guidelines. Try drinking all of your allowance at once, for instance. Or save it up for a month, take a couple of days off work, and then drink eighty-four units in one sitting. If you are married to a teetotaller, you can drink your partner's allowance too. Then you can sink thirty-five units a week on the grounds that you're drinking for two.

There have even been warnings about having sex in the summer. Not only can it put a strain on your heart, but in the grip of sun-induced passion and twenty-one units of lager you may forget to roll on your condom properly and so die of AIDS before the skin cancer gets you.

My advice is to treat the experts with the derision they deserve. If the Rubber Johnny Police want to spend the summer dressed in radiation suits, drinking Perrier and not getting their leg over –because by the time they've read the instructions on the side of the Durex packet three times and had a few practice unrollings, they've either run out of condoms or their partner has lost interest – that is entirely a matter for them. But when it comes to nannying, those of us who simply want to be left alone are fighting a losing battle.

In the summer of 1994, I wrote a column suggesting that it would only be a matter of time before the health fascists demanded government warnings on the side of sweet packets. A MARS A DAY DOESN'T HELP YOU WORK, REST AND PLAY, IT MAKES YOU FAT AND ROTS YOUR TEETH. HOPE YOU CHOKE ON IT, YOU GREEDY BASTARD was one of the slogans I imagined. Little did I know, as I embarked on my flight of fantasy, that the Mars advert was the subject of a complaint in the Independent Television Commission. An outfit called Action and Information On Sugars – whoever the hell they are – wanted the commercial banned. They alleged it was misleading and that there was no medical evidence to support the claim that a Mars a day helps you work, rest and play. The ITC spent fourteen months deliberating whether 'consumption of chocolate increased the production of serotonin, a substance in the brain which encourages sleep, relaxation and contentment. There were earnest discussions on whether the levels of sugar and hydrogenated vegetable fat were sufficient to generate enough energy to help you work and play. Eventually the commission concluded that 'there was no specific sense in which the consumption of a Mars Bar per day could be meaningfully said to be beneficial for these purposes'. It beats me how they managed to keep a straight face. Why do they humour these bastards?

The ITC rejected the complaint on the grounds that to ban the advert would be 'to carry literalism beyond any reasonable grounds justified by the needs of consumer protection'. In other words, they politely told Action and Information On Sugars to sod off and stop being so daft. Why they couldn't have done that fourteen months earlier is beyond me. I suppose they have to justify their existence somehow. God knows how much all this nonsense cost us.

Three million people every day buy Mars Bars. They do so because they like them, not because they believe they are gaining any medical benefit. Most of them would probably say Mars Bars do help them work, rest and play. Certainly they helped Mick Jagger and Marianne Faithful play, if not work and rest.

The ITC ruling did nothing to stop the madness. The campaign against sweets and sweet advertising has continued unabated. The puritans have tasted blood. At the beginning of February 1995, after a concerted campaign, The ITC caved in and announced new 'guidelines' banning adverts which encourage adults and children to eat too many sweets. It followed a similar decision the previous month by the Advertising Standards Authority, which regulates ads in newspapers, magazines and billboards. this is what an ITC spokeswoman told the Press Association: 'The new rules mean that all food advertisements must have regard to increasing public expectation that advertising in this sector should pay responsible attention to the health implications.

'In particular the new code outlaws creative treatments which could be seen as encouraging or condoning over-indulgence in products such as confectionery and those which disparage good nutritional practice.'

Evil, like beauty, is in the eye of the beholder. I wonder what the ITC makes of the Cadbury's Flake ad? You know, the one where the pouting, scantily-clad bimbette lovingly peels the wrapper off the crumbling confection and slides it between her lips. One man's blow-job now becomes another man's tooth decay, cholesterol and obesity under the new 'guidelines'. And what is the difference between setting out your stall and 'encouraging or condoning over-indulgence'? I don't know about you, but I don't think I've ever seen a chocolate advert which peddles the message:

'Eat 300 of our super-rich, sugar-enhanced bars and we absolutely guarantee that not only will you not put on a single ounce but you will get to screw Elle MacPherson into the bargain.' People are not stupid. Correction, people are stupid. But that should not be a subject for legislation. If adults want to eat their own body-weight in Milky Ways because they really do believe that it's so light that it's the sweet you can eat between meals without ruining your appetite, then they must be suffering from delusion or a serious eating disorder. Let them get on with it. Eventually they will be sick, or unable to fit into any of their clothes and they might put two and two together.

Back to the ITC ruling. You might have thought that the complainants would be dancing in the streets, celebrating their famous victory over the wicked forces of edible temptation with an extra helping of muesli and a foaming pint of Evian water. Not a bit of it. Here's the reaction of something calling itself the National Food Alliance, obviously the provisional wing of the RJP: 'The ITC has failed to address the cumulative advertising message to children, a message that overwhelmingly portrays fatty and sugary foods as attractive and desirable food choices,' said project officer Sue Dibb. I wouldn't want to be stuck next to her at a dinner party. Pass the carrot juice. And I suppose a fuck's out of the question, pet? And the National Consumer Council's acting director Robin Simpson said: 'We are disappointed that the ITC has decided not to deal with the sheer quantity and frequency of TV advertisements selling food and drink which is high in sugar and fat, especially adverts aimed at young children.' All I can say is that I'm glad he's not my dad. Daddy, daddy, can we go to McDonald's? Please, daddy, daddy. Shut up and eat your kelp.

Children do need protection, but that should be a job for

parents, not for the State. There's always been advertising for sweets. In a democratic, free society, with a market economy, companies should be allowed to advertise any product that it is legal to manufacture. What is the point of letting firms churn out Monster Munch and Milky Bars if you then try to stop them selling them? The truth of the matter is that kids like fast food, sticky buns and sweet drinks. And there's nothing wrong with letting them indulge – even over-indulge – from time to time. But the Confectionery Division of the Rubber Johnny Police don't want them to be allowed a little of what they fancy. Not once in a while, not ever.

This isn't about banning adverts, it's merely the opening salvo in a campaign to outlaw sweets altogether. Speaking of Milky Bars, it can only be a matter of time before the Rubber Johnny Police put out a contract on the Milky Bar Kid. After all, this character is to chocolate consumption what the Pied Piper was to the nuclear family. To be honest, I'm surprised the Kid wasn't assassinated long ago. It must have escaped the notice of the Commission for Racial Equality that the chocolate he was promoting was on the lighter shade of white. Still, mustn't tempt fate.

The trouble with all this hysteria is that it rubs off elsewhere. With predatory lawyers and appetite outreach co-ordinators poised to pounce on anyone selling pro-scribed food. Here's a classic example: I had a leaflet advertising a local restaurant offering a home-delivery service pushed through my door. In the fish section, next to PLAICE (with chips, peas, tomato, lettuce, and lemon) £2.30 and COD (with chips, peas, tomato, lettuce and cucumber) £2.50, there were a series of asterisks. After wondering why you get cucumber with cod and not with plaice – and pondering the inevitable confusion and distress which could be caused by trying to order plaice with cucumber – I looked to see what the asterisks denoted. Speciality of the house, perhaps? Recommended for vegetarians? Er, not as such. (*Please take care. May contain bone*), it warned. Why? Do the proprietors think we are so thick we do not realise that the fish have bones. I doubt it. More likely it is to protect them against the avalanche of writs under the Trades Descriptions Act from disgruntled customers and the council chip-shop safety gestapo.

'Oi, Doris. It didn't say nuffink about the bones, did it? Bastards. Lets get on to the Town Hall. We'll have them shut down.' Why stop there? Why not: (*Please take care. Polystyrene box is not edible*). Or: (*Please take care. Don't poke fork in your eyes*)? Whatever next? Government health warnings in neon lights outside Burger King reading: WARNING: THE SURGEON GENERAL HAS DECREED THAT FLAME-G ILLED WHOPPERS MAY BE DETRIMENTAL TO HEALTH, ESPECI-ALLY IF EATEN WITH FRENCH FRIES AND AN EXTRA-THICK STRAWBERRY MILKSHAKE. NOW PISS OFF DOWN THE HEALTH FOOD SHOP.

Of course, all this food fadism is a South-of-England, largely Metropolitan disease, infecting *Guardian* readers and professional complainers and prodnoses with nothing better to do. They'd get short shrift in Glasgow, for instance, where deep-fried pizza is the order of the day. And I wonder what the Advertising Standards Authority and the massed ranks of the cholesterol patrol would make of a sign I saw in a chip shop window in Blackpool, home of all things fried. It was advertising the *spécialité de la maison* – although it didn't quite put it like that – probably because there is no literal translation of 'Gutbuster Special'. This consisted of two beefburgers and two slices of processed cheese crammed into a white, processed bun and then deep-fried in lard. Served, naturally, with chips. It cost a very reasonable £1.99 and was advertised as a 'Recession Beater'. I remember watching two southern Labour Party activists – all knit-your-own breakfast and John Lennon glasses types – looking on in horror as the boilermakers' delegation queued two-deep to fill their boots. While there are still trenchermen in politics, there is still hope. Let's hope they washed down their feast with a couple of cans of Carlsberg Special Brew.

Carlsberg is probably not the best lager in the world. But the commercials are entertaining. Needless to say the RJP want them banned too. Probably the same people who want Mars Bars banned. I imagine they would like them replaced with commercials showing tramps and winos supping Special Brew in the gutter, with the slogan: CARLSBERG SPECIAL BREW, PROBABLY THE BEST LAGER IN THE WORLD FOR DOING YOUR BRAINS IN COMPLETELY, ROTTING YOUR LIVER, LOSING YOUR JOB AND ENDING UP IN A CARDBOARD BOX. But best not to tempt fate.

Let me give you another example, from one of my local pubs, the Maid of Muswell. Vic is an old-age pensioner who gets in the Maid most days for a couple of pints of Guinness and a small cigar, while he does the *Telegraph* crossword. He is a creature of habit. His order never varies. One day, Vic wandered into the Maid on his way to the legion and asked for a Guinness and a Hamlet. The barman pulled him his pint but said he couldn't sell him a single cigar. When Vic asked why, he was told: 'Europe'. The barman said that a directive had come from the brewery that individual cigars could no longer be sold because individual Hamlets don't carry health warnings. If he wanted a cigar he would have to buy a whole packet, which did carry a health warning. He explained that any barman selling a punter a single cigar could be subject to disciplinary action. Vic pointed out that the very same barman had sold him a single cigar the previous day. The barman agreed but said since then the pub had received a set of 'guidelines' from the brewery, designed to bring the Maid 'into line with Europe'. He could, however, sell him a Castella, on account of the fact that Castellas are big enough to have a health warning printed on the cellophane wrapper. Vic peered at the wrapper and said the warning was in such small type that he couldn't read it, not with his eyesight any road. The barman said that didn't matter. Just so long as the wrapper contained a health warning it was OK. There was no obligation for anyone to actually read it. Since Vic has been smoking for the best part of sixty years, he is well aware of the dangers or otherwise of cigars. As a free man, who fought in the war, he considers it his right to smoke himself to death if he so wishes. There really is no limit, is there? I hesitate to suggest that the next time Vic calls in for a pint and a small cigar, someone might refuse to serve him on the grounds that he can't prove he's over eighteen.

The only thing that you can be absolutely certain about is that this week's health warning will be contradicted by another survey at some date in the future. When we were kids, the official recommendation was to eat dairy products on the grounds that eggs, milk and butter were all good for you. By the time my kids were born, dairy products were 'proven' killers. In 1987, doctors at St Thomas's hospital in London recommended people to switch from saturated fats to polyunsaturated fats to lower cholesterol levels. In 1989, scientists said that polyunsaturated fats might actually raise, not lower, cholesterol. Consider a few other examples: In 1986, a study by Sir Denis Burkitt, a Nobel prizewinner, discovered that eating lots of fibre was the surest way of combating cholesterol. Four years later, another study at Harvard and Boston found that a high-fibre diet made no difference to cholesterol levels. In the meantime, sales of bran fibre, muesli and wholewheat bread had skyrocketed and doctors began to report an increased incidence of bowel and colon irregularities. Some people were eating so much fibre it was quite literally ripping their insides out. In fact, some doctors attribute so-called irritable bowel syndrome to unnecessary high-fibre diets. In 1990, the Health Education Authority recommended pregnant women to eat liver twice a week for the iron content. In October of that year, scientists at the Ministry of Agriculture warned pregnant women not to eat any liver, because it contains high levels of Vitamin A, which can cause birth defects. July 1986, the government warned that peanuts, and in particular peanut butter, can be harmful because of levels of a substance called atoxin. September 1992, doctors in the USA announced that peanut butter can stave off heart attacks and cure constipation. There's a whole book to be written on this kind of contradictory evidence. I'll leave that to someone else. But now that scientists have said that a double brandy or half a bottle of wine each day will do more to prevent heart attacks than a low cholesterol diet, what can we expect next – smoking sixty a day helps prevent lung cancer? Chocolate good for the teeth? It's no good. It will happen, as sure as eggs are now good for you again. You couldn't make it up.

LET THEM DRINK
PERRIER

In the wake of the row over huge pay rises for the former water board bosses, I received the following in a brown paper envelope:

Herewith the minutes of the last meeting of the privatised British Water Corporation, held in the banqueting suite of the Hotel de Posh, St Tropez.

APOLOGIES FOR ABSENCE

Sir Henry Goldrim, finance director.
The chairman asked if there had been any word of Sir Henry since he flew to Rio de Janeiro six months ago on a fact-finding mission, accompanied by his secretary, Miss Blowjob. Mr Laptop, company secretary, said funnily enough Lady Goldrim had been on the telephone asking the very same question. Sir Henry was obviously alive and well and, judging by his corporate American Express Gold Card bills, had apparently now decided to extend his fact-finding activities to the Acapulco Bay Racquets and Scuba Club.

Item One

The chairman inquired if the accounts department had managed to trace the £1 million shortfall which was discovered shortly after Sir Henry left the country on

business. The company secretary said there had obviously
been a computer error and proposed accounts could be
brought back into balance by putting an extra £5 on water
bills.
Passed unanimously

Item Two

Mr Rover-Sterling, the transport manager, reported that the
corporation's fleet of Jaguar Sovereigns was now almost
three months old and the ashtrays needed emptying. He
proposed replacing all vehicles immediately.

The chairman agreed and said that since the company was
no longer in public ownership there was no need to retain a
strict Buy British policy. He had always fancied a Merc, and
his good lady had her eye on a BMW convertible.

Board voted unanimously to purchase a new fleet of S-
Class Mercedes for all directors.

Item Three

New headquarters. The chairman said that the corporation
was in urgent need of more modern accommodation. The
existing premises dated back as far as 1989 and were
becoming increasingly overcrowded. There was only room
for four in his Jacuzzi and frankly he'd always considered
gold taps vulgar. Board voted unanimously to allocate up to
£150 million to the project and don't forget the swimming
pool.

Item Four

Chairman reported that the corporation's new £100 million
advertising campaign would be appearing in newspapers
and on TV next month.

Mr Laptop said he didn't want to be a spoilsport but why
did the corporation need to advertise? After all, it wasn't as if
consumers could buy their water from anyone else. Couldn't

the money be better spent on things like new office furniture, overseas conferences and pay rises?

Chairman explained that his brother ran an advertising agency and if Mr Laptop didn't ask silly bloody questions there might be a non-executive directorship in it for him.

Item Five

Mr Ringmain, the operations director, reported a growing number of complaints about the quality of water coming out of domestic taps. Consumers reported running brown baths and filling up their kettles with raw sewage. A gentleman on the Nelson Mandela estate had a crayfish swim into his sink the other day when he went to do the washing up.

Chairman said he shouldn't shout too loud or everyone would want one. (*Laughter*).

Item Six

Interim financial report, delivered in the absence of Sir Henry by his deputy, Mr Pocket-Calculator.

The corporation had made a record surplus of £750 million in the previous three months. Restructuring and down-sizing was progressing well. A further 30,000 maintenance workers had been sacked during the quarter and the savings achieved were already showing marked improvements, not least in the quality of the claret in the executive dining room. The chairman proposed that the hard work of all those involved should be rewarded. All directors' salaries should be increased by 150 per cent forthwith and treble share options all round.
Passed unanimously

Item Seven

Water charges. Although domestic charges had increased by 250 per cent over the previous three years, Mr Pocket-Calculator said they had still not kept pace with the cost of maintaining the corporate fleet of Lear Jets. He therefore suggested that a further supplementary rise of £50 per household be levied from August 1, which would make provision for golden handshakes.

He suggested that the press office be instructed to issue a statement to the media saying that this money was needed to combat the effects of the drought. Mr Laptop said what drought? It hadn't stopped raining since Christmas.

The chairman said sometimes he wondered about Mr Laptop and if there wasn't any further business he was off because he was late for a meeting down the coast at Nice of the Railtrack Board, to which he had been appointed by the minister in recognition of the outstanding success of the British Water Corporation.

Chairman asked company secretary to make a note to appoint the minister as non-executive director of the corporation if he was unlucky enough to fall off his perch in the reshuffle.

Company secretary said that the Water Consumers Council had written pointing out that any further increase in charges would make water too expensive for pensioners and others on fixed incomes. Chairman said let them drink Perrier. If anyone wanted him over the next six weeks he could be contacted via the Acapulco Bay Racquets and Scuba Club. *Miss Blowjob would know where he was*.

DON'T MENTION THE WAR

The Queen Mother has always struck me as a complete waste of space. And the line about her being the nation's favourite grandmother is frankly insulting to everyone else's grandmother. 'Well, she did visit the East End during the Blitz,' her fan club points out. So what. My grandmother *lived* in the East End during the Blitz. But I don't remember the Coldstream Guards turning up outside her window playing Happy Birthday. Nor did the state feel obliged to award her £100,000 a year out of public funds in perpetuity on her ninetieth birthday. Nevertheless, late in the day I began to warm to the old bird when it was reported that the Queen Mum had written to Channel 4 protesting about a documentary rubbishing Sir Arthur 'Bomber' Harris, the man who ordered the bombing of Dresden in the closing stages of the war in 1945. In her capacity as patron of the Bomber Command Association, she described Harris as 'an inspiring leader' and strongly criticised those who portray him as a bloodthirsty villain.

Sir Arthur was treated shamefully by the British Establishment and died without ever being awarded the peerage to which he was richly entitled. I've always been opposed to the honours system but, since one exists, it is an enduring disgrace that Sir Arthur was denied the ermine which adorns the shoulders of nonentities such as Lord Young,

Lord Owen and Lord Stevens. Harris was punished by those who seek to rewrite history, with the Germans portrayed as victims of Hitler as much as the peoples of the occupied countries and the residents of the East End and Coventry, who found themselves on the receiving end of the Luftwaffe's bombs.

We all know that German pilots were forced into their planes at gunpoint, don't we? How many times during the D-Day commemorations were we told that Britain was actually at war with the Nazis, not the Germans – as if the Nazis were an alien species beamed down from Planet Zanussi. Don't forget that in the last free election in 1933, 17 million Germans voted for Hitler. They knew perfectly well what his agenda was. How many Jamaican Nazis were there? How many Welsh Nazis? How many Outer Mongolian Nazis? Exactly.

By the time the revisionists have finished, the Germans will have been transformed from sadistic, warmongering mass-murderers into compassionate, peace-loving people unprovoked by the evil Winston Churchill and the blood-thirsty RAF. Just as future generations of Americans will think their nation was built by Ethiopian lesbians and Red Indians. Leaving aside the Falklands War, Dresden was the last piece of British foreign policy we can be proud of. But if you listen to the hand-wringing liberals you'd think it was a terrible war crime for which we are all collectively guilty. On the fiftieth anniversary of the raid, the *Guardian*'s Jonathan Steele wrote: 'The Americans have Hiroshima. We have Dresden . . . no reminder is more uncomfortable for the British.' There were countless other articles in the same vein, not just confined to the left-wing press. Simon Jenkins wept for Dresden in the *Spectator*, demonstrating yet again that when it comes to his list of priorities, people lag a long way behind buildings.

I don't feel in the slightest bit ashamed of what happened at Dresden and I suspect neither do millions of others, including the vast majority of readers of this book. My only regret is that we didn't do it sooner. And the Germans can think themselves damned lucky they weren't on the receiving end of an atomic bombardment. They certainly deserved it. I wasn't born until nine years after the end of the war. If it had gone the other way I probably wouldn't have been born at all. Members of my family were among those subjected to incessant bombing in the East End. Even if Dresden was not strategically crucial it made them feel better after being on the receiving end for years. And I don't suppose the relatives of all those British soldiers tortured and starved by the Japanese lost any sleep over Hiroshima, either.

It is important that my generation, my children's generation and my children's children's generation should be reminded of that. There is an Orwellian rewriting of history taking place, which seeks to portray the Germans and the Japanese as 'victims' of the war. They were no such thing. They were the aggressors. It shouldn't even be necessary to point that out, but it is an indication of how far things have become blurred that I feel I have to. As for the bombing of Dresden, just for the record, it is worth pointing out that a number of eminent military historians say that Dresden was strategically important. The city was a crucial link in the German communications system and was the site of vast marshalling yards and the centre of a road network assisting the movement of German troops. As for the war being nearly over, in February 1945 – when the bombing of Dresden took place – the Germans were still bombarding London with V2 rockets and claiming the lives of British civilians. And even if the war was nearly over, there is still a rock-solid case for exemplary punishment being meted out to the German population which had sustained and encouraged Hitler. A healthy dose of revenge is good for the soul.

At least the Germans have had the decency to admit their guilt and atone for it, something the Japanese never have. To this day the Japanese have not apologised for their war crimes and have convinced the younger generation that they were the victims of the Second World War. The Hiroshima museum is dedicated to perpetuating that myth. One of the finest leaders ever published by the *Sun* – in the days before I started to write a column for it – marked the death of Emperor Hirohito. '*Rot in hell, slant eyes,*' it reasoned. It almost caused an international diplomatic incident. Yet men like my wife's late grandfather, Harold Tuck, would have thoroughly approved. He certainly didn't accept the view of Japan as victim. To the day he died he would never remove his shirt in public – not even the beach – because of the terrible scars inflicted in a Japanese prisoner-of-war camp. British lawyers flew to Tokyo to demand compensation for the survivors of Japanese torture camps. I'd have thought Harold Tuck and men like him would have found that rather demeaning. God alone knows what they would have made of Lady Di bending the knee to the Japanese emperor during her quasi-state visit in early 1995. Far better that we should annually commemorate their ordeal by celebrating victory over Japan. The Government should declare every August 6 – the anniversary of the bombing – as Hiroshima Day and organise an appropriate programme of events –perhaps a fly-past above the Nissan factory in Sunderland and mushroom-growing contest in Hyde Park.

We have spent the last fifty years apologising for our part in winning the Second World War. The Germans and the Japanese have been the main beneficiaries. Here, take our car industry. Take our electronics industry. We're ever so sorry. Honest, we are. We didn't mean it. If the Nuremberg war crimes trials had been held in the present climate, the Germans and Japanese would have been awarded compensation for British aggression. And the Queen Mum would have been put in the dock, accused of leading the resistance.

The Japanese are still extremely touchy about Hiroshima. My agent, Alex Armitage of the Noel Gay Organisation, accompanied one of his other clients to Japan a couple of years ago, and was invited to make a speech to an assembly of theatrical dignitaries. He introduced himself and rattled off the usual innocuous platitudes and gratitudes. To his amazement his words were received with absolute silence, and he detected a sense of hostility towards him. Afterwards he asked one of his hosts if he had said something wrong. Diplomatically the man suggested that next time he was called upon to make a speech in Japan he might merely introduce himself as Alex Armitage, manager, and drop all reference to 'Enola Gay'.

If you're looking for conclusive proof that Britain as a nation has lost the plot completely, contrast the ceremonies at Dresden and Coventry cathedrals in the week of the fiftieth anniversary of the Dresden raid. The Germans got on with the business of remembering their dead in a typically understated, dignified fashion. Since 1945 they have gone out of their way to atone for the Nazi period and have dedicated themselves to rebuilding their nation and their international reputation through economic progress. Nowhere was that more apparent than at Dresden, a city emerging from four decades of communist oppression and beginning to share in the fruits of Germany's industrial success. Meanwhile in Coventry, once an industrial power-house, a motley collection of Trots, travellers, nutcases and animal sentimentalists crowded into the cathedral to deify a misguided young woman whose only contribution to society was to throw herself in front of a farm lorry.

We seem to have spent the last fifty years belittling our finest achievement and reducing our own society to ruins. We have razed our industrial base, destroyed our education system and thrown up a generation of decadent, unemployable welfare scroungers who think that animals are just as important as humans. If that's what they really think, they should have been in Dresden fifty years ago.

EPILOGUE

I'd like to end this book on an optimistic note. I'd like to be able to say things can only get better. But I'm a pessimist. I think the way in which the orthodoxy of the Left has embedded itself into the body politic is irreversible. The ratchet has gone too far. Even a right-wing Tory government will be powerless to reverse the decline. The chances of a US-style backlash are remote, particularly now that we are firmly on course to become part of a federal Europe. All we can do is rage against the machine and try to laugh about it.

I intend to be sitting at the back throwing bottles for some time to come. And occasionally the contents of those bottles will have been drunk to celebrate a small victory over the forces of political correctness. The only glimmer of hope is that the High Priests of PC will eventually come to their senses. There is a little encouraging evidence that this might happen. In an article in the *Spectator*, Melanie Phillips, the prominent *Guardian* writer – now moon-lighting on the Grauniad's Sunday sister the *Observer* – confessed that the Left might have got it all wrong. She admitted that political correctness has been a disaster and has betrayed a generation. Miss Phillips – presumably it's all right to call her Miss now – recognised that people like me have been telling the truth about the harm PC has caused in schools and in the social services. She even agreed that the Town Hall thought police in the racism, sexism, and disability units have ended up harming the very people they were intended to help, as well as stifling free speech.

When a prominent proselytiser of the Left puts her hands up maybe we should ask: what is going on at the *Guardian*? Can we soon expect 'Cripples – Don'tcha Just Hate 'Em' by Alan Rusbridger? Or 'Why Mandela the Terrorist Should be Strung Up' by Suzanne Moore? Or an editorial headed: 'Repatriate All Immigrants Now'? Will the *Guardian* jobs page soon be carrying ads reading 'White, able-bodied heterosexuals wanted. Smokers only need apply. No poofs or blacks'?

Nah, forget it. You couldn't make it up.